This item is the property of

Business Start Up @ Leeds Met

Leeds Metropolitan University

115 Leighton Hall, Beckett Park,

Leeds, LS6 3QS

For <u>Reference</u>

Use Only

Please do not remove

Business Start Up @ Leeds Met

MOVING TO SUSTAINABILITY

Moving to Sustainability

How to Keep Small Business Development
Centers Alive

Studies on centers in Poland, Hungary and the Czech Republic

*A publication of the Central European Small Business Enterprise
Development Commission*

Edited by

DANIEL S. FOGEL
Katz Graduate School of Business
University of Pittsburgh

MONIKA EDWARDS HARRISON
United States Small Business Administration

FRANK HOY
University of Texas at El Paso

Avebury

Aldershot • Brookfield USA • Hong Kong • Singapore • Sydney

338 - 040943 Mov

© D. S. Fogel 1995

All rights reserved. No part of this publication may be reproduced, stored in a retrieval system, or transmitted in any form or by any means, electronic, mechanical, photocopying, recording or otherwise without the prior permission of the publisher.

Published by
Avebury
Ashgate Publishing Limited
Gower House
Croft Road
Aldershot
Hants GU11 3HR
England

Ashgate Publishing Company
Old Post Road
Brookfield
Vermont 05036
USA

British Library Cataloguing in Publication Data

Moving to Sustainability: How to Keep
Small Business Development Centers Alive
    I. Fogel, Daniel S.
    338.642

ISBN 1 85972 297 0

Library of Congress Catalog Card Number: 95-80852

Printed and bound in Great Britain by
Ipswich Book Co. Ltd., Ipswich, Suffolk

Contents

Surveys of Small Business Activity

Case Studies on SBDCs

Preface

In 1990, the United States Congress passed legislation creating the Central European Small Business Enterprise Development Commission. The purpose of the Commission was to assist the governments of Poland, Hungary and the Czech Republic in supporting the growth and development of small businesses as their economies adjusted from controlled to free markets. This book is one component of that assistance.

The Commission was specifically charged with establishing demonstration projects in each country. The projects were to be modeled after the US Small Business Development Center program. The Commission worked with government officials, educational administrators and private sector representatives to launch Centers in each country. US funding was scheduled to last only through fiscal year 1995, after which the Centers were to be self-sustaining.

'Moving to sustainability' thus became a primary concern for the Centers, and a conference on the subject was held at the Czech Management Center in Celákovice, Czech Republic in April 1995. This book is a report on the conference. While it is not a comprehensive record, it includes many of the key presentations and covers virtually all of the major themes that were discussed.

The first section, **Models of Sustainability**, contains strategy recommendations from people who have served as technical advisers to the Centers and similar programs.

Surveys of Small Business Activity in the Czech Republic and Bulgaria come next. They provide a good overview of the general situation in these two countries.

The final section, **Case Studies on the SBDCs**, consists of progress reports from the directors of four of the Centers.

A brief introduction to the Commission follows this Preface and helps to set the stage for the main body of the book. Conference participants are listed at the end of the book.

This book should be useful to several kinds of readers:

- to anyone who is working to promote entrepreneurship and small business growth in emerging market economies.

- to students of economic development everywhere — especially those who are concerned with the tricky question of how an economic development program itself can be made economically viable.

- to anyone who cares about the progress of private enterprise in post-Communist nations.

For those who wish to replicate SBDC-type projects in other countries, the book offers a great deal of practical advice. More information can be obtained from the Office of International Trade of the US Small Business Administration, which provided headquarters space to the Commission, and from the participants in the Celákovice conference.

The Celákovice conference was an excellent opportunity to share information. The formal presentations, the discussions, and the friendships that were formed all contributed to everyone's learning and hope for the future.

Here is a summary of the most important points raised.

Summary of the 'Moving to Sustainability' Conference

We discovered that all small business development centers, regardless of stage of development and location, share common opportunities and challenges.

Financial considerations are primary. We agreed that no government unit or service, or combination thereof — either foreign or in the home country — will provide full funding for a Center. It is especially crucial to replace large central-government grants with funding drawn from the community as soon as possible.

- *Multiple funding sources* are needed, including the offering of services for revenue. Robert Pricer, of Public Access Inc. and the University of Wisconsin-Madison, proposed an optimum funding mix. He suggested that a Center seek to raise 25% of its funds in the form of direct contributions from local governments, banks and businesses, and the rest from a combination of fee-generating activities. These would consist of group workshops and seminars — including seminars offered through local trade associations, and custom-designed 'in-house' workshops for companies that can afford them — plus one-to-one consulting, and the sale of books and materials.

- Services for pay *are best offered in those areas of Center expertise.* To give an obvious example, small business centers are best at providing training, consulting, and materials that pertain to small business. SBDCs probably should not venture into ancillary businesses such as advertising or the sale of items such as software.

- Most participants agreed that a Center's director and associate director should spend a considerable amount of their time on marketing, through *direct personal calls* on businesses and government agencies that may want the Center's services. Less reliance should be placed on mailings and media advertising.

We concluded that personal marketing is more important in Central and Eastern Europe than in other parts of the world, since many prospective clients are not aware of the SBDC concept and have had little experience using consulting services.

- *Clarity of target markets* is critical. As in any business, the client mix is a major factor in the viability of an SBDC. Many participants suggested shifting away the focus on startup businesses, to work more with medium-sized companies that have growth potential and funds to pay for services. Centers could serve the startups mainly through group seminars — which are more affordable for the client and cost-effective for the Center — and only consult individually to startups that show great promise. Centers should probably have a screening process to identify these clients.

- One target market for ongoing consultation and partnership is *banking.* The SBDCs can be clearinghouses for banks, screening loan applications and working with potential borrowers to develop business plans. Banks would probably pay for this service, as it saves them time and money and helps them build solid loan portfolios. It also fits the mission of the Centers by helping businesses obtain financing.

Some participants suggested that SBDCs may want to focus on facilitating loans in certain industries, such as agriculture or light industry.

- *Shifting fixed costs to variable costs* will help the Centers survive, many people noted. For instance, the salaries of the director and associate director should be tied to the Center's income.

- At the same time, the *quality of personnel* is vital. Quality must be developed by paying good wages to good consultants, training people, and using experienced, responsive people to serve clients.

- *Networking* will help each Center sustain itself. Networks are linkages that provide clients, resources, visibility, and general support. Some important characteristics of networks are stability, uniqueness, routines and reciprocity.

Every Center director worries about the *stability* of linkages, especially with funders and key supporters. One way to increase stability is to include the contact person on a board, or directly in Center activities such as consulting or publishing.

The *uniqueness* of linkages should be evaluated from two viewpoints. First, each linkage takes time to manage and develop. Center directors should thus ask themselves how critical a particular linkage is to the Center's success. On the other hand, having a unique linkage may make the Center too dependent on a single source of support or funds. Thus, a Center may want to build into its network a redundancy that will help to reduce risk.

Routines are patterns of behavior that help people 'know how to act' when a situation arises. Establishing routines with linkage partners solidifies the relationship and creates a valuable sense of 'automatic' response. For example, after some time, the Centers would hope that banks and other agencies will send certain kinds of business to them as a matter of everyday practice. This relieves some of the pressure of having to look for new clients. A good question is: How can you establish such a routine? For example, what incentives could you offer a banker to encourage him or her to think of you constantly?

This brings us to the concept of *reciprocity*. The best linkages are those in which both partners feel they are getting value. Center directors could map their linkages, evaluating them in terms of the value for each partner. Those where the Center gives more than it receives, or vice versa, could be targets for change in the relationship.

- In networking, as in fund-raising, it is essential to cultivate local partners. Most Centers have found that universities, municipalities (especially the mayor's office), and a few medium-sized businesses were the most fruitful local partners.

- *Evaluation* is another area that contributes to sustainability. How can a center gather quality data on its performance? What formative and summative data will be used? Everyone agreed that an outside evaluator is critical, and that it is important to know certain standards in advance. Catherine Ashmore's paper (Chapter 4) has suggestions on evaluation criteria.

One benchmark is whether a Center grows faster than the average small business in its region. Participants felt that growth is the key to success!

- *Flexibility* is another characteristic of a sustainable Center. What do we mean by flexibility? A flexible Center has a variety of skills to meet a variety of client needs. Also, it has a certain degree of excess capacity — skills waiting to be used. This excess capacity is built by having relationships with various consultants, by being able to use university resources when needed, and by constantly training Center employees.

- *What should a Center be called?* Most participants were aware of using 'American' in the name as a marketing ploy (as in 'Polish-American Small Business Advisory Foundation'). Yet this precludes recognition from programs such as PHARE, a European Union assistance program.

- One final note from participants was that sustainability depends on a Center's ability to *do research* and *understand its fit with local conditions*. A research focus is important for several reasons. It creates constant innovation in the Center, keeps it current with market conditions, builds credibility with clients and people who refer clients, and builds capability in Center employees.

The Centers are in the business of propagating knowledge. Sustainable Centers do more than share existing knowledge with their clients. They generate new knowledge.

Acknowledgements

The editors would like to thank the many people who organized the conference and helped to create this book. Suzanne Etcheverry and Josephine Olson of the Czech Management Center were in charge at the conference site in Celákovice. They made our lives easy and treated us as honored guests. Jim Wingrove's service as Executive Officer of the Commission was invaluable, especially in organizing participants and making international arrangements. Mike Vargo's patient editing was instrumental; he was able to make sense of much of our writing and assure that others will be able to understand what we mean. The Joseph M. Katz Graduate School of Business at the University of Pittsburgh, the US Small Business Administration and the University of Texas at El Paso were most generous in allowing the Commissioners to devote time and other resources to this conference.

We also wish to thank the Association of American Universities, the Association of Small Business Development Centers, and the US Small Business Administration. The network we formed of US and Central European organizations made the entire Commission project a success.

Finally we are indebted to US Representative John LaFalce (D-NY), former Chairman of the House of Representatives Committee on Small Business, whose vision led to the creation of the Commission, and to Representative Jan Meyers (R-Kansas), current Chairman of the Committee on Small Business, for her strong and consistent support of the Commission's efforts.

We are not able to mention everyone who contributed to our efforts, but express our sincere hope that this book furthers the success of all those trying to develop small businesses in emerging markets. In closing, we offer a quote from Vaclav Havel that expresses the intent of our work in Central and Eastern Europe:

> *In a world of global civilization only those who are looking for a technical trick to save civilization need feel despair. But those who believe, in all modesty, in the mysterious power of their own human being ... have no reason to despair at all.*

The Central European Small Business Enterprise Development Commission (CESBEDC) and the Growth of the Centers

Adapted from the CESBEDC Annual Report for 1994

The Central European Small Business Enterprise Development Commission was established in 1990 by the US Congress, through Public Law 101-515. Its mandate was to assist Poland, Hungary, and the Czech and Slovak Federal Republic [now the Czech Republic and the Slovak Republic] in developing 'a self-sustaining system to provide management and technical assistance to small business owners' during the transition from socialist to market-oriented economies.

The legislation allocated three years of US government funding. Thus far the Commission has received four years of funding, although at lower rates than initially called for. (Total budget for fiscal years 1991 through 1994 was about $5.09 million.)

From the start, the Commission worked closely with national and local governments, trade associations, universities, and other groups in the US and Europe. Work began in fiscal 1991 with an assessment of the needs of small businesses in the designated countries. The Commission also evaluated the Small Business Development Center (SBDC) program, an American model that uses partnerships among universities, government, and the private sector to assist and counsel both existing and prospective small business owners. The research indicated substantial need in Central Europe for the types of services provided by SBDCs.

The Commission identified potential sites for SBDCs in Poland, Hungary, and the Czech and Slovak Federal Republic, and sought local institutions to host them. Criteria for selection included ability to respond quickly to small business needs, and ability to support the program after US involvement would end.

In fiscal 1992, management and technical assistance programs were established at three Centers in Poland — Warsaw, Gdansk, and Lódz — and at two in Hungary, at Debrecen and Pecs. Staff were hired and trained, and

1

furnishings, computers, and communications equipment were installed. Local nonprofit foundations and advisory boards were created to assist in operating the programs.

Potential sites were evaluated in the CSFR, but final selection was postponed to fiscal 1993 because of the changing political situation. After the country divided, the Commission decided to support planning for a Center at Brno in the Czech Republic, and organizational work began.

Meanwhile the Centers in Poland and Hungary had opened their doors. During their first year, the Polish Centers at Warsaw, Gdansk, and Lódz provided counseling to 1,116 clients and attracted 2,589 participants to seminars. Administrative standards were set, and the Commission monitored financial and operating procedures, providing support for improvements where needed. A review by the director of an American SBDC in Oregon commended the Polish program and made recommendations for the future.

Hungarian Centers in Debrecen and Pecs provided services and information to 1,164 people during their first year. The Commission's efforts focused on stabilizing service delivery, program development, and record-keeping and reporting. A consultant from the University of Wisconsin Enterprise Center provided training and assistance to the Center staffs.

In both countries, the Commission and its representatives worked to build strong national and local institutions that would be responsible for the Centers as they became self-sustaining. Emphasis was placed on financial and political commitments from governments, host institutions, and the small business community.

The Czech program opened in fiscal 1994. A limited SBDC demonstration project began operating in offices at Masaryk University in Brno. A National Advisory Council was formed, made up of Czech government officials and business leaders, and a Local Advisory Board provided oversight. During its first year the Brno program consisted primarily of seminars, although the Center offered a full range of services. Over 300 participants attended 24 seminars.

The Polish Centers in fiscal 1994 counseled 1,294 clients, attracted 2,539 participants to seminars, and made great progress toward sustainability. Full transition to Polish leadership was completed, with Commission representatives continuing to be available for advice. The program confirmed important financing agreements with government and private-sector organizations, and began charging fees for some services. On the national level, a grant was received to improve and expand the program. As a result of local sponsorship agreements, the Gdansk Center moved to the nearby city of Gdynia, and the Warsaw Center moved to the Polish Chamber of Commerce building.

Southern States Training Company, Inc. reviewed the program in Poland, pronouncing the initial phase a success and making recommendations for

2

advanced staff training and refined operating strategies. Another study, which included research on the quality and impact of Center services, found high satisfaction ratings among clients.

In Hungary in fiscal 1994, the Debrecen and Pecs Centers counseled 539 clients and held seminars attended by 798. To enlist support for continuing their work, the Centers concentrated on networking in the small business community and building relationships with organizations interested in economic development. The City Government host institutions continued their support, and other cooperative agreements were established. In a study done by the management and administration of the Centers, clients expressed high degrees of satisfaction with the services.

As fiscal year 1995 approached, Centers in all three countries were in the process of transition to full financial and management autonomy. With its mandate on the way to being fulfilled, the Central European Small Business Enterprise Development Commission, financed by the United States Congress, planned to cease its operations at the end of fiscal year 1995.

Central European Small Business Enterprise Development Commissioners and Staff

Frank Hoy, *Chairman*
Association of Small Business Development Centers

Monika E. Harrison, *Commissioner*
US Small Business Administration

Daniel S. Fogel, *Commissioner*
Association of American Universities

James Wingrove, *Executive Officer*
CESBED Commission
409 Third Street S.W.
Washington, D.C. 20416
phone 202-205-6662
fax 202-205-7592

US Representative John J. LaFalce (D-NY) was instrumental in establishing the CESBED Commission.

Part One
MODELS OF SUSTAINABILITY

1 Exactly What Are We Trying to 'Sustain'?

*From a letter sent to conference participants
in advance of the conference by*

*Daniel S. Fogel
CESBED Commissioner
from the Association of American Universities*

The title of this conference, 'Moving to Sustainability,' implies that we will be discussing how Small Business Development Centers (SBDCs) in Central and Eastern Europe will keep going after the withdrawal of foreign aid. One can expect us to discuss how SBDCs will obtain funds, establish themselves in their communities, and develop credibility as organizations that support small business development.

We will discuss these issues and try to discover how SBDCs can be sustained. Yet, we may not share a common definition of the term *sustainable*. Sustainable is not easily defined in terms of the development of new organizations such as the SBDCs. We may mean that an SBDC will remain as it was designed without change, thus sustaining itself. Or, we can mean that the intent of an SBDC is sustained, even if the organization changes over time. Or, we can mean that the larger community will take on the norms and values of small business development, sustaining an SBDC's intent even if the particular SBDC no longer exists.

Given this diversity of definitions, I'd like to offer some ideas that may help to clarify the sustainability concept as you contemplate your situation and the ideas you are preparing for the conference.

SBDCs are individual organizations that offer advice and support to small businesses within certain geographic areas. The Centers experience some of the same problems as do their clients — the Centers need to obtain capital, gain customers, hire employees, and maintain focus on their mission. Each Center must employ quality management practices to sustain the organization, practices that are often common to all small businesses. As every Center Director knows, the identification of causes of problems and management solutions is not easy nor always under the Center's control. I remember one US Center Director who said that his life was filled all day

7

with giving permission to solutions that were in search of problems. He hoped these solutions would match a problem — at least some of the time.

While this organization and management perspective is important — and while, for most of you, it is at the heart of what you want to gain from this conference, and the basis for being sustainable — I'd like to offer another idea of what is 'sustainable.' I believe that SBDCs are important as promoters of the norms and values of small business in Central and Eastern Europe. This aspect of SBDCs means that your organizations have value beyond your ability to meet the technical requirements of serving clients and staying in business. These additional values set you apart from other organizations and are equally as important to sustain as is your organization. Your job is to both build an organization and the *institution* of small business. In other words, if you are sustaining yourselves, you should consider how you will foster changes in values and normative relationships, and change the larger environment we can label 'small business.' You represent and will continue to represent the *institution of small business*.

Thus your task is much larger than having a functioning organization. Your task is to find ways to get others to adopt the idea that small businesses are important and that they have characteristics and needs different from larger organizations. How can you accomplish this task of sustaining the institution of small business? I'll offer three ways.

First, construct linkages or interdependencies with other relevant parts of your societies. These linkages are interorganizational ties that bring together entities that sustain the values of small businesses. Some of these linkages are with clients, small business associations, your board, government agencies and foreign funders. Other linkages are not so obvious, such as ties with the legal system and with government officials who will champion your Centers.

Second, you may want to benchmark your accomplishments in terms of viability and value in your environment. Several tests of your sustainability are your ability to survive, the environment's perception that your Center has value, your autonomy from foreign funders, the influence you wield, and the effect your Center has on other organizations. For example, to what extent does your Center become involved with local government policy development? The extent to which you are called upon for this advice is a measure of the extent of your influence.

Third, you can sustain yourself even if your organization ceases to exist as it is now configured. You have many organizational design choices, some of which will be different from the traditional American SBDC model. You may pursue one of these alternatives. Could you become an arm of the Chambers of Commerce? Could you be housed in a for-profit organization or an educational institution? Yet, you are sustainable in my mind only to the extent that you demonstrate and influence the norms and values of small businesses, regardless of your organizational form.

8

In summary, keep doing all of the things you need to do to keep your organization alive. But, keep in mind that your task is to develop small businesses and to influence the ways in which others share your values and support the institution of small business.

2 Applying the American SBDC Model to Central Europe

Frank Hoy
Chairman, Central European Small Business
Enterprise Development Commission
and
Dean, College of Business Administration
University of Texas at El Paso

Since World War II, multiple public sector programs have been initiated to facilitate and assist the creation and management of small businesses in the United States. The programs exist on the federal, state and local levels, often involving multi-level partnerships. The federal agency charged with aiding the small business community is the Small Business Administration (SBA). The SBA works with state Small Business Development Centers (SBDCs) and with other programs, such as the Service Corps of Retired Executives and the Small Business Institute program, to accomplish its mission of business development at the local level.

In recent years, representatives of the emerging democracies in Central Europe have been in contact with the US Congress, the SBA, and other organizations in America to learn how to stimulate entrepreneurship in environments that are shifting from planned to free market economies. The impact of small business creation and growth on job generation and broader economic development is well documented. The SBA's Office of Economic Research has constructed a database that permits longitudinal analyses of the US economy and has conducted and sponsored studies that show the significant role of the small business sector.

The Czech Republic, Hungary and Poland are currently undergoing rapid political and economic transformations. Each country converted to a socialist system following World War II and is now having to relearn free market economics. In the short term, this means institutional restructuring, rising unemployment, and many hardships for the people of Central Europe.

In order to assist in the transformation, the US Congress created the Central European Commission (see Exhibit 1). The Commission was charged with achieving three objectives in its first year:

1   to determine management and technical assistance needs of the small business sectors in the three designated countries;

2   to evaluate US small business assistance programs, particularly the various state Small Business Development Centers, to determine which most closely match the needs of the designated countries and may be replicated; and

3   to identify host institutions that might administer the programs.

During fiscal year 1991, the Commission awarded contracts to undertake research and assess needs in the three countries. In each country, the contractors conducted extensive interviews with small business owners and managers, government officials, representatives of educational institutions, business groups, and development assistance agencies. The contractors researched the needs of small businesses in each country, evaluated the SBA's SBDC programs to determine their applicability, and assessed potential host institutions for small business centers in Poland, Hungary and the Czech Republic. Examples of needs are listed in Exhibit 2.

Small Business Development Centers

There are many organizations in the United States that offer management and technical assistance to small businesses. One model that provides the essential elements of counseling, training and information services is the Small Business Development Center network. SBDCs are specified in the legislation establishing the Central European Commission as potentially replicable programs for this project.

The Small Business Development Center Program was begun in 1977, as a university-based extension effort. Its primary function was to utilize the expertise of the faculty and students of colleges and schools of business administration to help develop and implement management assistance and training programs. These outreach programs of the SBDC are designed to improve the equity, profit, and growth potential of small businesses and to develop jobs in the private sector.

The SBDC program is a management and technical assistance program designed to improve the economic climate of the United States through strengthening the contributions of small business to the economic system. It is a cooperative venture by local, state, and federal governments, universities and colleges, and the private sector.

One of the roles of SBDC counselors is to help clients identify obstacles to their success and differentiate those which clients can control from those they cannot. The Commission's research found several obstacles in Central Europe that individual business owners could not control (see Exhibit 3), but others that owners could overcome with expert assistance (see Exhibit 4).

Launching Assistance Centers in Central Europe

The enabling legislation for the Commission called for an 'educational institution in each designated Central European country' to develop SBDC-type programs. To qualify for participation in the program, an institution would have to:

1   obtain approval from its government,

2   provide financial support by the second year of the program, and

3   involve the private sector in delivering services.

A more detailed breakdown of host institution assessment criteria is included in Exhibit 5.

During fiscal year 1992, management and technical assistance programs were established at three SBCs in Poland (Warsaw, Gdansk, and Lódz) and at two SBCs in Hungary (Debrecen and Pecs). Staff were selected and trained, and each site was equipped with furnishings, computers, and communications equipment. Local non-profit foundations and advisory boards were created in the operation and overall implementation of the SBC program. In the Czech and Slovak Republic, site evaluations were completed for potential Small Business Centers. However, final site selection was postponed to fiscal year 1993 due to the fluidity of the political situation in the country.

A training program for the managers of the five centers was conducted at the state Small Business Development Center headquartered at the University of South Carolina. The training aimed to enhance basic understanding of all aspects of managing small businesses in a market economy, to develop the skills needed to manage small business centers and serve small business owners, and to increase personal awareness of the work ethic and attitudes for success in entrepreneurial ventures.

Directors and assistant directors from the centers participated in a six-week training session, which included intensive computer training, methods for standardizing and keeping records of client consultations, and sample guides and tools to manage day-to-day operations. Participants also received hands-on experience with SBDCs, visiting a different site each week. Mentors

13

worked with participants to enable them to prepare strategic business plans for their respective centers. Excerpts from the various business plans follow.

The mission of the Warsaw Small Business Advisory Center is to support economic development by providing managerial counseling services and ancillary technical support to small business firms and potential entrepreneurs in Warsaw and the Eastern part of Poland.

— Warsaw SBC Business Plan

Leveraging will be done using the resources of Chambers of Commerce, entrepreneurs' organizations, local authorities (especially for conference space), universities, high schools, research institutes, foundations and other organizations.

— Gdansk SBC Business Plan

Goals:
- Stimulate economic growth and business development.
- Provide high quality assistance to start-up, growing and existing small businesses.
- Establish a network with educational institutions and economic development organizations.
- Develop a consultant productivity measurement system.
- Expand programs aimed at stimulating economic growth.
- Establish and maintain professional image of Small Business Advisory Center's program and consultants.
- Promote education and small business research; establish and maintain a comprehensive library of business information sources.

— Lódz SBC Business Plan

During their first year of operation, Polish Small Business Centers in Warsaw, Gdansk, and Lódz provided counseling to 1,116 clients and attracted 2,589 participants to seminars. In Hungary, Debrecen and Pecs SBCs provided services and information to over 1,000 people during their initial year of operation.

On January 1, 1993, the Czech and Slovak Federal Republic separated into two countries: the Czech Republic and the Slovak Republic. Given assessment of the 1992 site evaluations in both republics, the Commission decided to support Masaryk University in Brno in establishing a Small Business Center. With the guidance of the Commission's consultant from the Hungary Small Business Center program, the officials of the university worked to set the foundation for the opening of a Center in 1994. A legal consortium of organizations, with the university as host institution, was established to sponsor the Small Business Development program.

14

Program Evaluation

SBDCs in the US have been subject to both internal and external evaluations since their inception. Many are evaluated in accordance with the policies of their respective state governments and/or host institutions. The SBA has contracted for a number of external evaluations. Several SBDCs instituted their own assessment and impact programs, some of which have been described in academic journals. In 1986, the SBA negotiated a process for on-site reviews with the Association for Small Business Development Centers. These reviews were instituted to satisfy a requirement imposed by the US Congress.

In Central Europe, each center collects data regarding counseling and training performance and reports results to the Commission. A list of one center's monitoring procedures is shown in Exhibit 6.

In 1994, comprehensive evaluations of the centers in Hungary and Poland were conducted. Research methodologies were adapted from the United States General Accounting Office (GAO), which had performed a nationwide assessment of US SBDCs in 1989. Results of the GAO analysis were compared with those in Hungary and Poland.

By most measures, the performance of the American centers exceeded that of Hungary and Poland. Two explanations for this finding are the relative inexperience of the Central European Centers and the lack of access to technology. On the whole, results of the assessments were quite positive.

Fulfilling a Mission

There are two guiding principles for US assistance to Central Europe: promoting democracy and encouraging free market systems. US policy has four objectives:

1   progress toward political pluralism,

2   progress toward economic reform,

3   enhanced respect for human rights, and

4   friendly relations with the United States.

The Central European Commission was created to encourage free market systems and to assist the Czech Republic, Hungary and Poland in making progress toward economic reform. Activities of the Commission have been conducted with the intent of cementing friendly relations with the United States.

Four criteria have been established by the US government to evaluate assistance programs.

1   concentration in areas where the US has a comparative advantage;

2   emphasis on practical, quick startup, immediate impact, and demonstration projects;

3   use of existing institutions rather than costly and time-consuming establishment of new institutions; and

4   coordination with other assistance programs.

The Commission's activities have met these requirements, as follows:

1   The SBDC program represents a model in which the US is the world's leader, and thus is a comparative advantage for American assistance.

2   Demonstration projects were quickly started, are practical in their functions and have had immediate impacts.

3   All centers were launched with the sponsorship of existing institutions.

4   Center activities have been coordinated with other US and Western European assistance programs and have leveraged the resources of other Central European organizations.

On September 30, 1995, the Central European Commission intends to conclude its mission of support for the demonstration projects. Its eventual success will be measured by the ability of the centers to sustain themselves and serve their countries.

Exhibit 1
US Legislation Creating CESBEDC
(the Central European Small Business
Enterprise Development Commission)

In the Congress of the United States:
Excerpt from Public Law 101-515 — Nov. 5, 1990

... SECTION 7. CENTRAL EUROPEAN ENTERPRISE DEVELOPMENT

The Small Business Act is amended by adding the following new section:
'Sec. 25. (a) There is hereby established a Central European Small Business Enterprise Development Commission (hereinafter in this section referred to as the 'Commision'). The Commission shall be comprised of a representative of each of the following: the Small Business Administration, the Association of American Universities, and the Association of Small Business Development Centers.

'(b) The Commission shall develop in Czechoslovakia, Poland and Hungary (hereinafter referred to as 'designated Central European countries') a self-sustaining system to provide management and technical assistance to small business owners.

'(1) Not later than 90 days after the effective date of this section, the Commission, in consultation with the Agency for International Development, shall enter a contract with one or more entities to —

'(A) determine the needs of small businesses in the designated Central European countries for management and technical assistance;

'(B) evaluate appropriate Small Business Development Center programs which might be replicated in order to meet the needs of each of such countries and

'(C) identify and assess the capability of educational institutions in each such country to develop a Small Business Development Center type program.

'(2) Not later than 18 months after the effective date of this section, the Commission shall review the recommendations submitted to it and shall formulate and contract for the establishment of a three-year management and technical assistance demonstration program.

'(c) In order to be eligible to participate, the educational institution in each designated Central European country shall:

'(1) obtain the prior approval of the government to conduct the program;

'(2) agree to provide partial financial support for the program, either directly or indirectly, during the second and third years of the demonstration program; and

'(3) agree to obtain private sector involvement in the delivery of assistance under the program.

'(d) The Commission shall meet and organize not later than 30 days after the date of enactment of this section.

'(e) Members of the Commission shall serve without pay, except they shall be entitled to reimbursement for travel, subsistence, and other necessary expenses incurred by them in carrying out their functions in the same manner as persons employed intermittently in the Federal Government are allowed expenses under section 5703 of title 5, United States Code.

'(f) Two Commissioners shall constitute a quorum for the transaction of business. Meetings shall be at the call of the Chairperson who shall be elected by the Members of the Commission.

'(g) The Commission shall not have any authority to appoint staff, but upon request of the Chairperson, the head of any Federal department or agency may detail, on a reimbursable basis, any of the personnel of such department or agency to the Commission to assist in carrying out the Commission's functions under this section without regard to section 3341 of title 5 of the United States Code. The Administrator of the General Services Administration shall provide, on a reimbursable basis, such administrative support services as the Commission may request.

'(h) The Commission shall report to Congress not later than December 1, 1991, and annually thereafter, on the progress in carrying out the provisions of this section.

'(i) There are hereby authorized to be appropriated to the Small Business Administration the sum of $3,000,000 for fiscal year 1991, $5,000,000 for fiscal year 1992 and $8,000,000 for fiscal year 1993 to carry out the provisions of this section. Such sums shall be disbursed by the Small Business Administration as requested by the Commission and may remain available until expended. Any authority to enter contracts or other spending authority provided for in this section is subject to amounts provided for in advance in appropriations Acts.'

Exhibit 2
Management and Technical Needs of Small Businesses

How to start and organize a small business

How to establish contact with foreign investors, and gain access to foreign markets and technology

How to negotiate joint venture or licensing contracts

How to gain access to information on legal and financial rules and an understanding of how they affect business

How to deal with foreign markets (customs regulations, prices, tariffs, transportation costs, etc.)

How to access Western data banks for contacts and market information

How and where to obtain credit and venture capital

How to obtain information on new technologies, especially computer and related MIS techniques

How to gain access to adequate physical space for business operations

How to deal with the banking system and establish creditworthiness in the absence of adequate collateral

How to do market research

Exhibit 3
Obstacles Beyond the Control of Business Owners

Uncertain economic climate

Lack of access to capital and credit

Lack of market-oriented business techniques and infrastructure (accountants, lawyers, bankers, etc.)

Evolving and uncertain legal systems (for instance, lacking clearly established property rights, or a reliable way to enforce contracts and resolve disputes)

Over-regulation and other red tape, especially affecting business startup

Inadequate physical space for commercial and production activities

Inadequate business infrastructure such as telephones, communications equipment and computers

Lack of government support for small business development

Fragmentation of asset ownership

Uncertain and burdensome taxation system, especially for employers

Absence of an infrastructure of business development facilities

Hostility toward and distrust of entrepreneurs among the public

Uncertainty regarding the pace of political reform

Opposition by managers and workers in some state-owned enterprises

Lack of banking services

Exhibit 4
Obstacles Within the Control of Business Owners

Lack of sales and, especially, marketing capacity

Weak knowledge of business planning, especially financial planning

Lack of management, commercial and entrepreneurial skills and experience

Poor and inappropriate organization, work facilities and equipment

Obsolete equipment and technologies

Unmotivated workers

Lack of access to markets

Lack of knowledge of investment capital

Business Start Up @ Leeds Met

Exhibit 5
Criteria for Host Institution Selection

Site Category:

Academic Institution
University level   Technical school   Other
Enrollment   Faculty   Curriculum

Small Business Association / Chamber of Commerce / Incubator
National or regional affiliation
Bylaws
Membership

Local Council Facility / Community Center / Other

General Capabilities Assessment

1   Existing business development programs or activities / perceived effectiveness of these programs.

2   History of prior cooperative program efforts with government / likelihood of government site approval.

3   Quality, quantity and small business orientation of resources: personnel / physical plant / equipment.

4   Nature of institution's existing financial resources: procedural controls / potential additional financial resources.

5   Ability to acquire, administer and implement outside assistance / outside funding.

6   Capability and geographic accessibility for outreach with small business community / potential to head network of subcenters and/or satellite locations.

7   Ability to contribute to the economic growth of the community being served.

8   Predisposition regarding host status for demonstration project.

Anticipated Structure

1   Administrative entity / organization chart

2   Advisory board function

3   Personnel: faculty / students / paid staff / organization officials / private consultants / other

4   Facilities: equipment / computer networks / library / other

5   Days / hours of operation

6   Dues / fees / contracts / agreements

7   Oversight structure / reports / reviews / audit

Exhibit 6
Typical Monitoring Procedures

- Each client is asked to write an evaluation of the SBAC services.

- Each consultant is required to prepare and submit all necessary records, requests for assistance and performance forms.

- Each consultant is to prepare a report noting his/her billable hours, and those spent with each client.

- The Center Director will monitor the activity records of the staff and others who may be enlisted to assist.

- Patterns of standardized experiences will be developed with other Centers.

- The performance and schedule of each consultant will be tracked by the Center secretary.

- The Center Director will conduct informal evaluations of staff and consultants on a monthly basis.

3 A Game Plan for Sustainability: Proven Strategies for Central European Management Development Centers

Robert W. Pricer, Public Access, Inc. and University of Wisconsin-Madison

Ralph Blackman, President, Public Access, Inc.

Introduction

Small Business Development Centers were established in Poland and Hungary, using the US SBDC model, by the Central European Small Business Enterprise Development Commission of the US Congress. The Centers were to be a three-year demonstration project funded by the US government with continuation funding provided by Polish and Hungarian sources following Commission support.

The Polish and Hungarian Small Business Development Centers have been very successful, providing both quality and quantity of service beyond that expected when the project was launched. However, US funding has lagged behind the level originally anticipated, and the Centers have struggled to maintain service levels with what is generally agreed to be inadequate levels of funding.

The lack of sufficient funding for the Centers precluded the establishment of a demonstration SBDC in the Czech Republic. In place of a full SBDC, a minimal amount of money was provided to a single Czech Center for one year for the establishment of a service program. Even with limited funding, this Center, located within the structure of Masaryk University, has been very successful and is providing a full range of services to small business owners and managers.

When the original demonstration period of three years was established by the US Congress, it was assumed that the transition to a market economy would be smooth and rapid in Central Europe. Unfortunately, this optimism has not been matched by the transition process and all three countries — Poland, Hungary and the Czech Republic — have experienced severe hardship as reality has taught that moving to market mechanisms will be long and painful.

With the rewards of free enterprise not yet realized in Central Europe, and with political instability, the prospect of government continuation funding for any of the Centers is bleak, to say the least. Socialists, including many former Communists, have been elected to power in both Poland and Hungary and the political polls in the Czech Republic indicate that the same may happen there. It is no secret that the Socialists are not supportive of using limited government revenues for activities designed to strengthen the private sector, and this places the Centers in a difficult position in terms of securing continuation funding.[1]

It is in this environment of difficult funding that this paper is written, suggesting strategies for sustaining the Centers and their important work. However, it is our belief that the Centers will need to revise their mission or domain statements to accomplish the objective of full funding. Originally the Centers were established to provide open access to small business owners and managers, or to those thinking of entering business, for management training and business counseling services. Now, the mission must be changed to include the need to generate sufficient revenue to cover projected expenses. This will require higher fees for services and a shifting of efforts to serving slightly larger, more established firms. The obvious negative impact of this strategy will be the elimination of most services to those small business owners, or those wanting to start a business, who are unable to afford the fees.

In the case of the Hungarian Centers, this change in mission is complicated because the municipal sponsors were promised a program that would serve the small businesses of their communities. Thus, a change in mission may result in a withdrawal of city support. At the very least, each advisory board will need to approve any change in mission, because the Hungarian Centers were designed to provide for local 'ownership' of the program.

The strategies suggested in this paper are based on the successful transition to sustainability of the CIFAG Management Development Center in Lisbon, Portugal. This Center was established with US funds to train managers of Portugal's newly privatized businesses in the late 1970s. (The country's businesses had been nationalized after the coup of 1976 that brought Socialists to power. When they were replaced with a centrist government in 1978, privatization began and this led to the establishment of CIFAG in 1979.) CIFAG started with total support and eventually become self-supporting with no government money of any kind. The lessons of this process have been adapted to the Central European situation. It is our hope that this will provide some useful suggestions for the Center Directors as they design and implement their own sustainability plans.

A New Mission

The first step in designing a sustainability plan is to recognize that full funding is not likely to be provided by any single government unit or combination of government units. The result is the need for a mission statement that reflects this fact. The new mission must include the requirement that significant revenue be generated through fees for services, information and materials.

Also, any Center located in a university (e.g., the Czech Center) should administratively move to an independent structure or foundation. In all the countries of Central Europe, universities are under intense financial pressures and will be unable to provide direct financial support to the Centers. In addition, any fees or other income generated by university-based Centers would be at risk as the universities attempt to meet their own escalating expenses. (This would likely take the form of 'charging' for services such as space and support activities, items normally contributed by a Center sponsor, to justify moving money out of the program.)

The university situation can be illustrated by looking at Hungary, where the higher education development plan calls for nearly a doubling of enrollments by the year 2000, without increasing the budgets of universities. In fact, the recent budget crisis in Hungary has led to significant cutbacks in university budgets. This situation is complicated by the plan, partially implemented, that will result in larger, more efficient educational units. The head of the Higher Education Research Division of the Ministry of Education, Gustav Serfozo, has been reported as saying, 'The battlefield is now at the universities.' We have been told by rectors that Hungarian universities are the wrong place for management development center efforts, given the current budget situation and uncertainty over reorganization.[2]

Universities in all the countries of Central Europe are in turmoil and they are not good homes for the Centers. For this reason, the mission statement must include a provision that the Center is an administratively independent unit that can receive fees and determine the use of this service-generated income.

When discussing the role of universities in management training, it is important to understand some of the differences between US and Central European universities. The undesirability of establishing Central European management development centers in universities was clearly documented in a survey of Hungarian business owners. Only 8 per cent indicated that management development programs should be hosted by universities, with the largest number, 39 per cent, indicating that 'trade or business association offices' would be the best location.[3]

This negative feeling about universities may be reinforced now that Socialists have returned to power in the Hungarian National Elections of May 1994 and the Hungarian Municipal Elections of December 1994.

Similar election results have occurred in Poland and are probable in the Czech Republic.

Solution to the University Dilemma

The undesirability of universities as host institutions creates a real problem for the Centers, because the universities have both the knowledge and human resource base needed for effective management development services. For this reason, the Centers will need to identify, and contract for, the services of the most effective faculty and staff at universities. The mission statement must include a section indicating that university faculty members and staff will be the primary service providers of the Centers. These services should be provided on a contractual basis as needed by Center clients.

Shifting Fixed Costs to Variable Costs

One of the fundamental adjustments the Centers must make to reach sustainability is the shifting of fixed costs to variable costs. This strategy allows a Center to lower its breakeven point significantly and to minimize the risk of operating at a deficit. The largest expense of the Centers is personnel, both administrative and for the direct delivery of services. Therefore, payment for all but minimal administrative duties must be put on a contractual basis whereby the service provider is paid a percentage of actual fees received. The mission statement must clearly reflect this payment mechanism, as it is the foundation for fiscal stability during fluctuating economic periods.

The Sustainability Plan

Because full direct program funding is unlikely, a Center needs to first look at the budget required to meet its administrative and program expenses. As expenses will vary among Centers, this paper will use the assumed figure of US $150,000 as the total annual operating budget needed by a Center. While this is an assumption, we believe that each of the Centers could operate on this amount, and the plans suggested here can be modified to meet the market and funding sources available to each program.

Therefore, we assume each Center will require $150,000 per year to fully replace US funding if quality service is to continue.

The Projected Revenue Budget

In projecting a realistic revenue budget, it is extremely important to be conservative and to build flexibility into the estimates, to allow for adjustments needed to balance the final budget. Based on our experience in Portugal, we believe it is essential that some local government and private direct support of the Center be secured. In Portugal, CIFAG became completely self-supporting without any government or other direct funding. While this was a remarkable achievement, the result was that CIFAG became a 'private' company supplying management development services. Had some government funding remained, CIFAG would have been integrated into the economic development plans and decisions of Portugal, and local 'political' identity with the program would have been developed.

For this reason, we suggest that 25 per cent of the total budget — or $37,500 — be generated from municipal and local private sources. This will provide local 'ownership' of the program and ensure that the Center remains a force for coordinating and integrating management development services in its service area.

1   Local Funding from Municipal and Private Sources:
    a   Municipal Budget Support = $25,000
    b   Bank Contributions = $5,000
    c   Business Contributions = $7,500

This projected amount seems to be realistic, based on our experience with CIFAG and with the Centers in Hungary. Both municipal governments in Hungary, Pecs and Debrecen, have made significant investments in their SBDC programs. Both mayors have requested at least this amount of direct city funding for their SBDC programs, and funding is very likely because each city will receive ongoing services with an annual cost of $150,000 for its $25,000 investment. However, given the budget situation and Socialist majorities in the City Assemblies, additional funding is not highly probable.

Banks can be expected to make contributions of $5,000 in aggregate, especially if they can refer small business clients to the Center for loan application assistance and business planning services. However, given the conservative nature of Hungarian banks, contributions beyond this level are not likely.

Private businesses, especially larger firms, are a good source of limited support. The probability of contributions will increase if the SBDC is perceived as being a source of reliable economic information, and as playing a public advocacy role for free enterprise. With market reforms being openly questioned by many, the need for a strong 'independent' voice for free enterprise is recognized by most companies.

2   In-House Workshops:
     Total = $30,000

The general low-fee workshops of the Centers have gained a reputation for high quality and value. As a consequence, the Centers can contact the owners of larger companies and offer to design workshops specifically for a particular company. The sessions would be held on the premises of the company for its managers. This is a very cost-effective way for large firms to train managers, and the Centers can contract for the teaching of the sessions with qualified faculty on a per-session basis. It is conservatively estimated that 25 three-day in-house workshops can be provided each year, at a fee of $1,200 per workshop.

3   Association Seminar Services:
     Total = $25,000

In Central Europe, many business and trade associations were formerly part of national or local government with membership being obligatory. With reform, these associations need to find ways to serve their members as affiliation is becoming, or has become, voluntary. The association managers are largely unable to organize and present meaningful seminars, and many will welcome the opportunity to develop a strategic alliance for this purpose with the local Center. The Center would develop and offer the agreed-upon seminar for members; the fees would be split between the association and the Center with the larger proportion going to the Center.

4   Workshops and Seminars:
     Total = $50,000

The seminars offered by the Centers to business owners and managers have been very successful and a modest fee has been charged for them. With sustainability an issue, fees need to be raised and the number of workshops increased. Participants for these workshops will come from medium-size and larger businesses from the region served by the Center. This will require personal selling of the educational service, by directly calling on firms and discussing these offerings along with in-house programs. A Center will need to offer approximately 90 workshops of varying length with an average fee of $35 per attendee. This will require about 1,400 attendees or an average of just under 16 per workshop.

5   One-on-One Counseling:
     Total = $5,000

Because a majority of effort will be redirected to workshops and seminars to raise fee income, there will be limited time available for one-on-one counseling. The counseling that is provided will be on a 'cost sharing' basis. That is, clients will be expected to pay a portion of the cost of the service. For example, the Centers will charge for loan packaging and other measurable services provided to individual businesses. It is estimated that each Center will generate 500 hours of billable counseling at $10 per hour.

6   Publication Sales:
     Total = $2,500

The Centers in the Czech Republic and Hungary have written and published books on topics of interest to small businesses, and this should continue after Commission funding. The $2,500 revenue estimate is very conservative; actual sales should be much higher.

Estimates for all of the categories above are based on our knowledge of the Hungarian Centers and the experience of CIFAG in Portugal. The amounts can be altered to fit the sustainability plans developed by each Center, but these examples provide a good starting point. It should be emphasized that each plan will need to include detailed program and service descriptions if implementation is to be successful.

Implications

The development and implementation of a successful plan for self-support of the SBDC Centers in Central Europe will have some implications that need to be fully understood. The Centers must change their mission statements and shift their activities to revenue-generating services and programs.

To accomplish the revenue generation objective, the Center Directors and Associate Directors will need to redirect their efforts significantly. Specifically, they will have to dedicate a minimum of 50 per cent of their time to the direct marketing of Center services and programs. The experience of CIFAG suggests that the only effective way to market a Center's services is to make direct, personal calls on businesses and government agencies that might want manager training, or information, or counseling services.

It will no longer be enough to publicize the Center through mailings or media advertisements. With higher fees and increased programming, the only way projected participation and revenue can be achieved is through direct personal marketing. In short, the Center Director and Associate Director will need to identify the organizations and appropriate decision makers and call on all of these in their service area. *If the situation in Central Europe is similar to that of Portugal, this required change in activity will be the key to success. Yet it can be anticipated that Center staff will resist this change, as most are comfortable with their current duties and job expectations.* However, the Directors and Associate Directors must understand that success can be achieved only if they change their daily activities to place emphasis on direct marketing.

Because fees must be raised to reach sustainability, the target audience for Center programs and services will shift to medium- and larger-size businesses, along with governmental units, within the service area. This means that service to small businesses and individuals who want to start a business will diminish, if not be eliminated. For many Center Directors, this will be difficult to accept, as past services and programs were largely designed for those who could not afford to pay market rates.

The new client description will need to be carefully defined, with the ability to pay the needed fee being the major criterion. It will be important for the Centers not located in a major urban area of the country to keep in mind that they probably cannot compete with established management development programs outside of their service territory. For example, in Hungary the two SBDC programs are located outside of Budapest. The Budapest area is well serviced by others and it would be a mistake to try to attract significant trade from this urban area. However, it would be a good strategy to try to persuade managers within their service areas not to travel to Budapest for programs when they can receive the same, or better, quality through the local Center at lower travel costs and program fees.

If startup and very small businesses are to be served, it will have to be on a paying basis through group instruction. For example, it might be possible to continue to offer courses in starting a business or writing a business plan with a reduced fee if the number of participants makes the program feasible. As a general rule, a Center will need to generate about $550 for each workshop or seminar if sustainability is to be achieved. For example, this revenue can be generated by charging $35 for a seminar and attracting an enrollment of 16 people — or by charging a fee of $15 and drawing about 40 people. Therefore, the key to small business workshops and seminars will be the development of topics that attract large numbers of participants.

The final implication of the implementation of a sustainability plan is the shifting of a Center's fixed costs to variable costs! This will lower the breakeven point and allow the Center to survive downturns in demand. As the largest fixed cost of the Centers is salary, this cost needs to be placed on a variable expense basis.

Specifically, it is recommended that the salary of the Director and Associate Director be placed on a percent-of-revenue-generated basis. The Center secretary and office expenses would be covered by the municipal, business and bank contributions. Because the Director and Associate Director would be assuming income risk based on revenues generated, they should have the opportunity to receive a bonus if income exceeds projections with expenses staying within budget. They would have the ability to receive a 'draw' each month to meet basic living expenses, but this amount would be included within the percentage-of-revenue income they would receive.

The shifting of fixed costs to variable cost by placing the major portion of salaries on a percent-of-revenue-generated basis is essential for long-term survivability. While this is certain to create uncertainty and stress in the beginning, the higher income possible under the arrangement should provide an incentive for the key activities of the Director and Associate Director.

Conclusion

The sustainability plan described in this paper is a call for the total restructuring of the Central European Small Business Development Centers. While it may seem radical, it is required given the total withdrawal of Central European Small Business Enterprise Development Commission funding at the end of the current fiscal year.

This plan is based on the experience of a similar center located in Portugal that faced the same elimination of funding and had a similar startup mission. We hope our suggestions will be of use to the Centers and their governing boards as sustainability plans are developed and implemented.

Public Access, Inc., stands ready to assist the Centers in the transformation process through advice or the review of sustainability plans.

Notes

1   The CESBEDC Centers are not the only programs that have been impacted by this slower-than-expected transition process. In both Hungary and the Czech Republic, the EU PHARE Management Development Centers have faced severe funding difficulties. In a March 9, 1995 front page story in the IPOZ national newspaper, it was reported that the Hungarian LEA PHARE Centers were unable to meet their increasing revenue budget requirement and that their future is in question. In the Czech Republic, the PHARE Centers have either closed or are in the process of closing.

2   For a description of the turmoil in the universities of Hungary, see Woodward, C., 'Hungary Moves to Streamline Its Universities and Eliminate Vestiges of the Soviet-Style System,' *Chronicle of Higher Education*, September 23, 1992, p. A35 to A37.

3   Avenal Associates Hungary Team, *A Study and Recommendations for Small Business Development Projects in Hungary*, September 1, 1991, p. 52.

4 A Preliminary View of the World Bank Micro-Enterprise Project in Poland

Dr. M. Catherine Ashmore
Director, International Enterprise Academy
Center on Education and Training for Employment
The Ohio State University

Piotr Korynski
Center on Education and Training for Employment
The Ohio State University

Introduction

Entrepreneurship is considered a major road to freedom among those who see the way of the next century in Central Europe. Developing a sense of self-reliance and the skills to create strong local economies has been our goal since 1990.

According to an article in the *Warsaw Voice*, Dec. 4, 1994:

> Small and medium-sized businesses play a basic role in any [market] economy. They create new jobs and radically reduce unemployment. They also increase the rate and scope of innovative processes and stimulate local and regional development. In the Polish economy, which is undergoing a fast transformation from central planning to market orientation, the development of small and medium-sized business can additionally help increase the rate and scope of privatization. It can also help increase the competitiveness of Polish businesses in domestic and foreign markets.

Entrepreneurship education and technical assistance in Poland and Hungary has been the focus of a number of projects funded by US AID and the World Bank since 1990. In each of these projects, we have sought ways to empower our local counterparts and provide materials adapted to their culture and translated into their language. Generally our first priority was to

35

provide programs for the unemployed because of the immense impact of this new group on political, social, and economic changes.

Sustainability of the projects after external funding is completed is the most essential feature of any program. Everyone has heard that it is better to teach a hungry man how to fish than to give him a free fish. So we have sought to teach Polish and Hungarians how to be leaders in the development of their own entrepreneurial societies.

The 3 Dimensions of Sustainability

We define sustainability as the interrelationship of three factors that impact the future of the initiative:

Financial — the ability to bring in new sources of income on a continuous basis, while keeping costs within an appropriate level.

Institutional — commitment to the project by an established organization that provides a location, low-cost or no-cost resources, and available personnel. All these are part of what is necessary to give any project the image of strength and long-term viability to those who choose to use its services.

Managerial — the leadership capacity and project-related skills of those managing the project, and their commitment to stay with the project and train others over time.

10 Keys to Creating Sustainability

Before discussing one case study of sustainability in our current project in Poland, we wish to suggest that there are 10 basic premises of sustainability. In designing any externally funded project we must consider which of these concepts will apply.

1   **Creating Institutions versus Providing Programs.** The purpose of development is not (or at least not only) to supply programs to an arbitrarily chosen group of people. It is also imperative to create an institutional framework for provision of different services, which will be able to respond to business needs and opportunities.

2   **The Program Itself Is Not Enough.** It is not the program itself but the institution's capacity to use it and adjust it to the changing economic environment that matters. The program (educational, financial etc)

36

constitutes the ultimate service to the target audience. But the program must be internalized by the organization, so that it takes ownership of it and delivers it as its own.

3   **Institutions Have Their Own Interests and Incentives.** The interests and incentives of the staff constitute the major driving force of the institution and create its image. Assistance efforts must concentrate on developing interests and incentives that will be compatible with the goals of programs and serve the needs of the target audience. For example, if you want to serve youth, you need to know how to work with young people, be truly interested in it, and not only do it because there is donor money available.

4   **Targeted Groups Must Be Incorporated in the Institution's Mission.** Targeting special groups (such as youth or women) who might otherwise be omitted has been a traditional approach. It remains important but must be related to the abilities of an institution to serve the identified audience in a systematic way over a longer period of time. If an institution is only able to sustain its efforts for a short time and then go out of business, then the whole idea of assistance is not credible and the target audience will not believe in it nor participate in its activities.

What incentive would unemployed people have to repay loans if they could easily predict that the loan fund will go out of business in six months? None, of course. This is a clear waste of resources, and a missed opportunity for positive intervention to change the economic conditions of the target group.

5   **Institutions Must Learn To Be 'Tough.'** The idea of development is to introduce a positive intervention into the economic system that will have spillover effects. We expect businesses to start and grow, efficiency to improve, jobs to be created, standard of living to improve, dependence on welfare programs to be reduced, and so forth. There must be clearly defined economic and social outcomes that will pay off the initial investment in the target group. Development is not charity and this should be recognized by development institutions. It is a vehicle for independence, not for reinforcing dependence.

6   **Institutions Must Adopt A Commercial Approach.** Institutions must learn to provide their services and operate in a businesslike way, so that their income can cover costs in the long run. They must learn to identify all of their costs, so that they really know what they must be able to cover. It is too easy to become dependent on the donor agency's support and not realize how expensive some activities can be. Institutions must plan for

income in the future and learn to be independent.

7 **Institutions Must Be Realistic and Focused.** The goals of the institution must lie within its capacity to achieve, and be realistic in terms of ability to provide impact on the target group. Well-designed programs must specify types of assistance and amount of assistance (in number of hours, number of clients, length of assistance, etc.) as well as specify things that they do not do. It is important to understand limits and set them in advance. For example, although we work with unemployed persons, we provide only business assistance and would refer clients to other service providers for other types of help.

8 **Institutions Should Be Professional and Efficient.** A professional institution is one that can adjust and survive in a dynamic environment. The business of providing 'business support services' is fast-growing and competitive in Eastern and Central Europe. It requires that the staff deliver services by proven and efficient methodologies. Efficiency relates to cost-effectiveness of service delivery. Institutions should establish benchmarks for admissible cost per outcome in a particular situation, then develop methods to obtain this efficiency.

9 **Institutions Must Fit Into Local Initiatives.** Institutions must be created that fit with local development initiatives in terms of targets, approaches, methods, type of funding, length of programs, etc. Each new initiative should serve the needs of the local community and not harm initiatives already in place. For example, bringing in subsidized training programs could prevent an existing program from reaching sustainability — not because the existing program was poorly designed, but because it was undermined by other 'cheap' programs.

10 **People are the Most Valuable Parts of Every Institution.** Only committed people make things happen. Local development institutions are usually small and limited in their operations. But they must have staff with vision and courage to go against the mainstream, to be able to create opportunities for positive changes in the community.

The challenge for American consultants in Eastern and Central Europe was to transfer knowledge and experience to their counterparts while respecting their personal expertise and abilities to figure things out for themselves. Our approach was always a team planning approach, in which we discovered everyone's abilities and learned to solve problems together. When we began our work we learned it was always easier to define the problem than to look for options to solve it. The process of decision-making was critical to the success of our teams and the ultimate transfer of expertise.

The World Bank Micro-Enterprise Project

As technical assistance providers for the Polish Ministry of Labor's program to help the unemployed, we face the biggest challenge of sustainability yet. In a period of about two years we are endeavoring to establish 30 small business assistance centers, 30 incubators, and 30 loan funds.

At present [April 1995], in our first year, we have established 24 centers, 12 incubators, and 10 loan funds in small and medium-sized communities all over Poland. This immense project has only begun, yet we feel a sense of success in developing sustainability of the sites from the very beginning. The design of the program focused on sustainability factors. These have been enhanced by decisions of the technical-assistance consultant team as the project progressed. We are working with seven Polish consultants and three Americans whose expertise is directed to training the local managers and establishing their sites to provide services to small business owners and the unemployed.

Financial Sustainability

This factor will become more important, as original investments from the World Bank and the Ministry of Labor have been used to get the program started. In the program design we addressed this issue in the following ways:

- Local site selection was based on commitments from the local government and local Labor office to support the project. It requires matching money on an ongoing basis to cover the costs of staff in the local center.

- Local Labor offices committed to using some of their training money for the programs offered by the centers. This is designed to cover some of the costs of staff both now and in the future.

- Each center is required to develop a business plan that will determine how it will find resources to cover its costs, with at least three-year projections. Consultants have trained the centers to develop these plans and are helping in their completion.

- Other organizations are encouraged to work cooperatively with the centers to bring additional resources.

- Equipment purchased for the centers can be used to provide rented services to local business owners. These can include office equipment as well as tools and machines needed on a limited basis to improve the technology of individual businesses.

- Local Labor offices can provide contract workers to the new business centers and incubators, subsidizing the salaries of the workers and reducing costs.

- Training by the project staff in all types of business skills is available to the local site managers at no cost. Also they can obtain individual assistance from the project consultants at no cost.

- Books, videos, software, training materials, and other resources have been provided to the centers at no cost. These may also be used by clients of the centers. Thus information on small business is available in Polish in even the smaller cities in Poland.

- The loan fund provided by the World Bank and Ministry of Labor charges clients for the use of money at the same or higher rates than banks, and thus covers inflation and costs of operation.

- The incubators charge their clients rent for the use of property that has been given to the project by the city, thus covering operational costs for project staff in the local sites. The agreement with the city is for a minimum of 10 years' use of the property.

Institutional Sustainability

This factor was part of the basis for selection of each of the local sites. It is important to access all available resources in the community, to make the center as strong as possible.

- Each site submitted a proposal to the local Labor office showing the use of matching resources in the community. The local Labor office selected the one best proposal from its area, with whom it was willing to be a partner. After that, the regional Labor offices chose the three best proposals in each of the 49 voivodships in Poland. And from these 140+ proposals, the Ministry chose the sites that are part of the project. This process was designed to find the strongest institutions to manage the project as well as finding the areas with the most unemployment.

- Each site was required to establish a new foundation or association specifically to handle the responsibilities of the project before it was given funds to operate the project. Thus we insured that sites were legally allowed to carry out the necessary work.

- An SBAC was required to have an agreement for use of its property for at least three years; an incubator for at least 10 years.

- Each site has a slightly different organizational structure, but in general this includes a council of city representatives who oversee the work of the project and assist the manager in solving problems as they arise. Thus each city feels ownership for its local center or incubator.

- The individual site managers have formed an association of all sites across Poland to ensure that they communicate with each other and assist each other. This arrangement gives a strong national image to the project.

Managerial Sustainability

This factor is the most difficult to control, because skilled managers have many career opportunities. However, we feel this is the most critical factor in maintaining the program on a long-term basis. Our approach to developing this expertise is as follows:

- Many training sessions have been provided by American and Polish consultants for the local site managers.

- Where the candidates for the local leadership position provided in the proposal are not adequate for the job, we have recommended obtaining replacements. We have interviewed and assisted in the selection of new managers.

- To help the local site managers develop management skills adequate to run their centers and incubators, we have developed a list of competencies for our consultants to evaluate each of the local managers. The attached chart shows that we have addressed management, marketing and financial skills using outcomes in each center as our basis of evaluation. The summary of all of these reports gives an interesting basis of comparison among the sites. We use the same format for evaluation regardless of whether the site is an SBAC, EDF, or incubator; thus we have a method to evaluate the growth of all managers in the program.

- The incubator team has developed a model business plan and provided it on computer disc to each site, to help local managers individualize the plan to their needs.

- Assistance is being provided to all sites in setting up record-keeping processes, so that all sites will keep the same types of data and it can be combined for analysis of the entire project.

- The technical assistance consultants have written model procedure guides to assist all of the sites in setting up their own management systems.

Summary

At this time Poland is in the beginning stages of development of 90 total new managers, to help the unemployed get started in business in 30 of the voivodships. The program aims to support the development of expertise in the management of 30 small business advisory centers (SBACs), 30 enterprise development funds (EDFs) and 30 business incubators. The sites that were chosen are in 30 different counties, located in small towns as well as larger ones. The Ministry of Labor and Social Policy has invested heavily in this project because it provides a cost-effective solution to the large unemployment caused by the privatization of state-owned businesses.

By the end of 1996 we will be better able to judge the sustainability of all the small business assistance center sites, and we recognize the difficulty of the challenge ahead.

5 Sustainability of a Small Business Support Center: What It Takes

Donald L. Pressley
USAID Representative to Poland

It is a sincere pleasure to join you in your deliberations concerning the role of small business support centers in the transformation of Central and Eastern Europe from central, command economies to market-oriented economies governed by democratically elected governments. I am particularly pleased that those of us involved with the Poland program have been given the opportunity to share our experiences. As the USAID Representative to Poland, I must admit my bias and tell you that I think before this conference is over, you will see the impressive contribution the Polish participants are making to the growth of small business in Poland.

I believe the conference is particularly timely and is focused on the right issues. The story of US Government assistance to Central and Eastern Europe is a three-act drama, and Act One is now over.

Act One started with the dissolution of command, centralized systems across Central and Eastern Europe. There was tremendous enthusiasm, support, and commitment by US institutions responding to the spectacle of Central and East Europeans struggling to take charge of their own destiny. The world watched in awe as the people of Central Europe began to influence the political, social, and economic reformation sweeping across this part of the world. From an assistance perspective, US institutions were the main characters in Act One, and the plot was their enthusiastic launching of assistance activities. As the curtain closes on Act One, we can applaud those players and congratulate them on an incredibly swift job of responding to developments in this part of the world.

This conference is the intermission between Acts One and Two. Act Two will be more complicated and intricate, as we bring to center stage the indigenous institutions that are the real story of this aspect of development in Central Europe. In Act Two, we must find ways to shift the international, US-based institutions to the role of supporting actors who work with their

European partners as true equals capable of developing and sustaining their own activities, rather than viewing indigenous institutions primarily as beneficiaries or recipients of foreign assistance.

In Act Three, we foreigners get to sing our swan songs and gracefully retire to the wings. The curtain will come down and rise again on a new Central Europe, no longer asking for foreign assistance of any kind, ready and willing to play its own mature part in solving the problems of tomorrow's world.

But now we are at the interregnum between Acts One and Two. As the playwriters of this particular play, we must think through the way in which the foreign partners will turn over the lead to the institutions of Central and Eastern Europe.

In examining this issue of the role of indigenous institutions — particularly institutions that support the growth of small and medium-sized enterprises (SMEs) — I think there are five questions that need to be answered:

1   Are small business support activities needed in Central Europe at all?

2   If so, what types of support activities are needed?

3   Will these same types of activities still be needed beyond the time frame of international funding?

4   If so, which activities are the most likely to be sustainable and why?

5   If Small Business Development Centers are among those likely to be sustainable, what will it take to make them sustainable?

Let me make a brief attempt to answer some of these questions, using Poland as the basis since I am most familiar with that situation.

1   Are Support Activities Needed?

A superficial look at the first question — should we be doing anything at all? — could lead us at first to answer, 'No.'

Poland has had an impressive economic growth rate of roughly 5 per cent per year for almost three years. The share of GNP contributed by the private sector has grown from less than 10 per cent to more than 50 per cent in less than five years. Maybe we should just be sure we don't get in the way of the private sector, which obviously is able to handle itself very well, thank you.

These macro statistics, though, mask the micro situation. Small businesses typically have a high failure rate even in the most favorable business climates. Hence, an even higher rate of business formation must be constantly

44

encouraged, simply to offset the turnover. Moreover, small business activity thus far has been focused primarily on trading products, particularly imported consumer products. Today more small businesses are being established to produce (rather than just trade) goods. This will require more sophisticated management than simply selling does, in areas such as product design, production control, quality assurance, marketing, finance, etc. Also, restructuring is still occurring, with major employment implications for sectors such as coal mining. There is an entire second wave of would-be businesspeople whose entrepreneurial skills will need to be developed and nurtured.

When one considers these and other factors, I think the conclusion is that support for small and medium businesses should definitely remain a priority.

2   What Types of Activities?

The next question is what types of support are needed. In Poland, we've identified three types of assistance targeted to the support of SMEs, and we think of them in pyramidal form.

At the broad base of the pyramid are services like the Small Business Development Centers, providing advisory services to SMEs directly. We also include the following among the USAID-funded activities in this category: International Executive Service Corps (IESC), Citizens' Democracy Corps (CDC), MBA Enterprise Corps, Volunteers in Overseas Cooperative Assistance (VOCA), and Polish Business Advisory Service (PBAS).

At the center of the pyramid are financial services providing loans and equity to SMEs. There are basically three USAID-funded organizations in this category: Enterprise Credit Corporation (ECC), Fundusz-Mikro, and CARE Small Business Assistance Corporation (CARESBAC).

At the top of the pyramid are policy support and government lobbying activities, intended to help government be aware of and understand the needs of SMEs and, hopefully, modify the enabling environment to be more supportive of SME growth. In this category we fund two activities: GEMINI and the Polish Federation of Independent Entrepreneurs (PFIE).

3   Will These Same Types of Activities Still Be Needed?

The Polish government already has answered the question of whether these types of activities will be needed beyond the time frame of US government assistance. It has set up its own Foundation for the Development of SMEs with the mandate to try to promote and fund (if needed) small business support activities in each of these areas. Clearly the current government in Poland understands the importance of SMEs to its economic growth and is pursuing a positive policy in that regard. Even though foreign financing is decreasing for SME support, in-country governmental support at the national, regional and local level can and should be a real and increasing possibility.

4 Which Activities Are Most Likely to Be Sustainable?

Whether all these various activities will be sustainable over the long run is yet another question. Let's look at examples from each of the three areas I've mentioned, to see some of the sustainability issues that can be encountered at each level of my 'pyramid.'

First Example: PBAS

The Polish Business Advisory Service (PBAS) is funded by a number of donors and was set up to help medium-sized Polish companies obtain financing from various sources of capital, in particular foreign capital. PBAS found this 'matchmaking' to be much more difficult than expected, and thus expanded its role to include more general business support — such as consulting with companies on business plans, corporate organization, financial systems and other business development activities, as well as on developing financing proposals.

The particular niche that PBAS has chosen is to develop and strengthen the Polish consulting firm community. An in-depth evaluation of PBAS concluded that PBAS should continue this approach, which in turn should be an example and an inspiration for the Polish consulting industry. At the same time, the evaluation concluded that PBAS probably could not stay on this course without continuing financial support. If foreign donors like USAID cannot continue to provide that support, then an organization like PBAS will have to look to other in-country sources.

Second Example: ECC

In the financing area, let me mention the Polish American Enterprise Fund's Enterprise Credit Corporation, its subsidiary to make loans to SMEs. The ECC has been a phenomenal success, disbursing over $90 million in loans with a loan loss write-off of less than 3 per cent. The ECC currently operates eight branches and is planning on expanding its banking operations to SMEs through franchise agreement with the First Polish-American Bank in Krakow, Poland.

Third Example: PFIE

The third area — policy advocacy — is exemplified by the work of the Polish Federation of Independent Entrepreneurs (PFIE). PFIE is a new entity funded by USAID and intended to be a grass-roots organization lobbying on behalf of SMEs. It plans to finance its operations through dues paid by the SMEs. Since we're all aware of how little capital SMEs have for this type of activity, PFIE will have to get lots of members and will have to prove its worth very rapidly.

5 Are SBDCs Likely to Be Sustainable, And What Will It Take?

At this stage, I'm sure that those of you still awake are asking yourselves, 'What does this all mean for Small Business Development Centers?'

My point is that business support activities are needed; they are recognized as valuable by the government of Poland as well as by the US government; but they can and should take many different forms. Equally important, the road to sustainability has many divergences that each country — and perhaps even each Center — will have to figure out for itself.

On the other hand, I do think there are some consistent lessons we've learned that can be applied to your Diogenes-like search for truth in this regard. All viable support organizations are going to have (I believe) certain common characteristics that should be addressed in one way or another:

- A Clear Message
- A Popular Base of Support
- A Search for Excellence
- A Business Orientation
- A Capacity for Flexibility

A Clear Message

No organization can afford to lose its sense of purpose and no organization can effectively 'sell' itself without a clear statement as to who it is, what it does and why it's doing what it does.

A Popular Base of Support

This will vary by type of organization. For a business, it is the customer orientation that would apply. For a business support institution, it is identifying your constituency and ensuring that whoever 'they' are, they understand you and support you.

In other words, you must identify who should receive your clear message and you must be sure they understand and support what you are doing. You may be supported by many outsiders, but without your own clearly-targeted base of support, all the others, in the end, won't matter.

'Support,' by the way, can take many and varied forms, but if your constituency isn't willing to contribute some share of financial support, then you should consider very carefully whether you have their true support or not.

A Search for Excellence

If you aren't striving to be the best, you probably won't even survive. This is the hard message of the marketplace. If you think you're the best, then set your own goals for excellence and work to improve even more. Complacency leads to stagnation, which leads to death. It has happened to the most successful organization, and it's a lesson that can never be forgotten.

A Business Orientation

Every organization, no matter how laudable its objectives, has to be businesslike. It has to have good business plans; it has to understand cost elements and how to keep them down; it has to understand where and how to raise revenues.

I have deliberately not focused on financial viability as the only or even principal aspect of sustainability, because I firmly believe that financing is not the only issue. On the other hand, let's be honest, no organization can afford to ignore the business of carrying out its activities. USAID, for example, is a transitory source of financing. We want to, and we will, do all we can, but our resources are limited and as I noted before, our time in Central and Eastern Europe is limited.

In-country sources of financing (with rare exception) should be your target, and capitalizing on the business aspects of what you do should be considered. UNICEF cards, for example, are a great resource generator and have the additional benefit of keeping UNICEF's message constantly in the forefront. Look for ways to be financially viable from the start and don't be hesitant to recognize that your ability to do good depends in part on your ability to do well.

Those of you from Central and Eastern Europe know all too well how fast events can move, and how rapidly our assumptions for the future can be overtaken by events. Change can be a wonderful thing, but only six years ago most of us could not even have believed the reality of where Central Europe is today.

My point is that you have to be able to deal with change and you have to be able to adjust in order to accommodate it. Today's formula for success may be antiquated by tomorrow. Your quest for excellence will have to take into account this need to be flexible, or it won't work.

Conclusion

I have given you a very basic list of factors. I'm sure they are not new ideas to any of you. I'm also sure that in your workshops at this conference, you will have far better, more detailed ideas to discuss. Yet without constant attention to the basics, none of these organizations will get very far.

I hope that you continue to have a very successful conference and that you can continue to find what it takes for small business assistance centers in Central and Eastern Europe to become sustainable, most successful organizations.

Part Two
SURVEYS OF
SMALL BUSINESS ACTIVITY

6 Small Businesses and the SBDC in the Czech Republic

Miroslav Foret
Czech Republic SBDC,
Masaryk University, Brno

Michael Dolezal
Faculty of Economics and Administration,
Masaryk University, Brno

Background: the Czech Economy from 1948 to 1989

The era of socialism eliminated privately owned SMEs (small and medium-sized enterprises) from the Czech economy. From 1948 to 1989, all means of production were owned by the government. There were national enterprises (*národní podniky*), which usually were big companies controlled by various ministeries, while smaller ones were influenced by various state institutions on the regional level. Each of them had its own management as well.

The other form of ownership was the cooperative system. The cooperative society or *druzstvo* was typical in agriculture, in services such as shoe repair, and in small-scale manufacturing (for instance, of gardening equipment or household appliances). The advantage of this system was a better and closer rapport with customers. But both systems had to adhere to goals set by the national five-year plans for prescribed outputs, turnover, achievements of the workers, etc.

A minor change was introduced at the beginning of 1988. The Parliament passed two bills, Nos. 1/1988 and 2/1988 Sb., allowing those who were interested to obtain 'Municipal National Committee permission to provide activities for the benefit of citizens' (*Povolení národního vyboru k cinnosti ve prospéch obyvatelstva*). The holder of this permit could employ only himself; he could not hire other labor. Under such a license one could have a 'one-man show,' for example servicing washing machines. The serviceman's price list was subject to approval of the local authorities but obtaining spare parts, transport, and equipment was up to him. For women there were opportunities to work as dressmakers, furriers, etc. The conditions, however, were strict and not many used the chance. The financial reward was nearly the same as working for a company, plus one had the responsibilities of a 'private' business. But at the time, this was a ray of hope.

Since 1990, the year after the 'Velvet Revolution' of 1989, there has been evidence of the re-establishment and recovery of small business.

Difficulties Faced By SMEs

Despite having a simple organizational structure and flexibility — which are considerable advantages — SMEs also have certain disadvantages. They have limited access to capital, higher production costs (since machines often are not used to 100 per cent capacity), and less chance to obtain rebates for buying in quantity. Other problems include operating only in local markets, difficulty penetrating markets abroad, and limited funds for research and development.

Specific barriers for SMEs in the transition economy of the Czech Republic include the following :

- There has been a delay in passing bills important for running SMEs. The first commercial laws created in 1990 were sub-optimal; the Parliament has made fast but often slapdash work of new legislation.

- Any business needs a well-developed infrastructure: telecommunication lines, a wide range of banking services, transportation networks, consultancy. The help of government here may be indirect, but it is necessary.

- Under communist rule there was no chance to accumulate capital in a legal way. Hence, there was a lack of funds for establishing new businesses. Unavailability of capital usually tops the list of problems in any poll of enterprenuers.

- Other problems include: a lack of qualified employees for functions such as accounting and marketing, a shortage of skilled workers, low level of knowledge of foreign languages, a lack of business ethics, and a bureaucratic approach on the part of many state authorites.

Small Businesses from 1990 to 1993

Because of the lack of information technology and databases, we are short of information on SMEs from 1990 to 1993. Several sources have been investigated, some of which had to be adjusted (due to the split of Czechoslovakia into two countries in 1993) to get data as accurate as possible.

In 1991 the process of 'small privatization' began in the form of auctions of smaller businesses. At the same time, people retrieved property confiscated by the Communists via the process of restitution. In September 1991 there were 897,282 privately owned businesses. We can say that nearly all would meet the description of SMEs.

Data released by the Czech Statistical Bureau (CSU) in November 1992 showed an increase in the number of businesses to 975,860. And during that year, a survey of the top 10 fields for entrepreneurs was made:

Field	Number of Entrepreneurial Businesses (1992)
Building/construction	174,679
Commercial services (unspecified)	171,062
Retailing & repair	153,124
Accommodations & food service	55,225
Metallurgy, metalworking	49,397
Agriculture (small farms) & gamekeeping	36,292
Rental	35,420
Transportation & delivery	32,293
(Ready-made) clothing	31,260
Other	237,108

At the beginning of 1993 some changes took place. First, a new value-added tax was imposed. (There are two VAT rates, 5 per cent and 22 per cent.) Second, social security and health insurance terms caused business conditions to deteriorate, especially for self-employment. Approximately 100,000 dropped their licenses.

However, reasonable estimates of privately-owned businesses in December 1993 showed yet another increase, to about 1,200,000. Moreover, the share of GNP produced by the nonstate sector grew dramatically (see Graph 1 at the end of this report). The activity of the small and medium-sized business sector is demonstrated by Graph 2, which shows the number of private companies in the seven counties of the Czech Republic (the nonstate sector in Graph 2 includes both co-ops and private firms). An estimate of future development is shown in Graph 3.

The latest statistical data show the increasing importance of small business in the Czech Republic in 1994. We have 856,551 sole proprietorships registered, and 76,813 limited liability companies. These are regarded as the most important privately owned businesses, and SBDC activity focuses on them.

The Czech Republic SBDC in Brno

The conditions, development and perspectives of the Czech Republic Small Business Development Center in Brno are rather different from those of SBDCs elsewhere. In 1991 we began as a Consultancy and Education Center in the Faculty of Economics and Adminstration at Masaryk University, providing services not only for small startup business but for traditional large engineering and textile factories, public administration offices, etc. In the summer of 1993, an agreement between CESBEDC (the Central European Small Business Enterprise Development Commission) and Masaryk University was signed, and our SBDC was established.

Our financial situation is much worse than that of the SBDCs in Hungary or Poland. Our CESBEDC support is very limited. Since we are not able to offer one-on-one consulting to large numbers of entrepreneurs, we have tried to help as many as possible by using more seminars, participation in trade fairs, and media outreach, especially through business newspapers and magazines. We also have published two books: *And What About The Market?* (1993) and *Communication With The Public* (1995). The first one sold out very quickly.

We have good relationships with the Ministry of Economy of the Czech Republic (headed by Minister Karel Dyba) and also with the Brno Town Hall (through its Department of Economic Development), Brno Chamber of Commerce, Brno Business Innovation Center, the Czech Republic Design Center and other organizations.

We use four primary forms of communication with our clients:

- Seminars are popular. Last year (1994) there were nearly 30 seminars, attended by a total of more than 300 entrepreneurs.

- One-to-one consulting is very often conducted over longer periods of time (e.g., several weeks) to help clients solve their problems. We helped about 30 entrepreneurs in this way.

- Correspondence and telephone calls allow us to work with entrepreneurs in other towns and regions, such as Ostrava, Hradec Králové, and Prague. We handled 20 cases by mail or phone.

- Published materials — including books and articles in newspapers and magazines — are widely circulated, with hundreds of pieces sold thus far.

Although our conditions are different from those in Hungary or Poland, the problems of our clients are similar. They need help with marketing and market research; with business plans and with financial analysis. The advantage of our SBDC is very close contact with University faculty members. They participate as the experts in our work.

In 1995 we plan more one-to-one consulting as our financial situation improves and we become more experienced at solving our clients' problems. In many seminars last year, we told our entrepreneurs about business in the United States. For some of them the US market is very attractive; therefore this year we would like to prepare a book on the problems and requirements of exporting to the US. We hope that previous CESBEDC support of our SBDC could also have some positive effects for US business.

**Graph 1
Share in the GNP**
(nonstate sector)

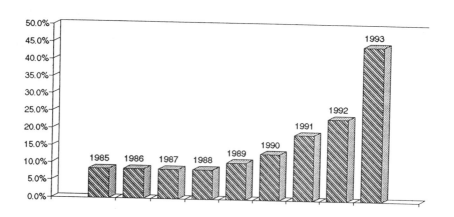

**Graph 2
Number of private companies
in counties in the Czech Republic**

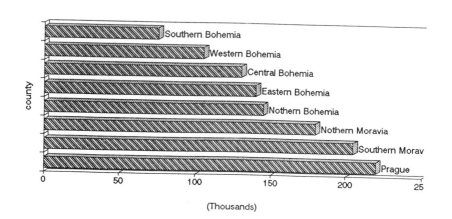

(Thousands)

Graph 3
The Estimate of the Future Development

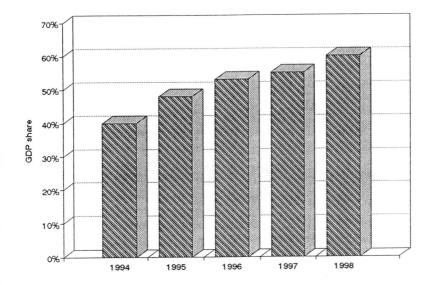

7 Small Business Development in Bulgaria

Mitko Dimitrov, PhD
Institute of Economics of the Bulgarian Academy of Sciences

Kiril Todorov, PhD
Department of Industrial Business and Entrepreneurship
University of National and World Economy, Sofia, Bulgaria

This paper presents a general picture of small business development in Bulgaria since 1990, as well as some preliminary results from a study of 120 SMEs carried out in the ESBID research project (Entrepreneurship and Small Business Development in Bulgaria 1993-1996).

Tendencies in the Development of Small Business

The size, structure and distribution of business enterprises in Bulgaria at the end of the 1980s were typical of centralized socialist economies: Large enterprises predominated. Small enterprises were found occasionally; they were started primarily to fulfill social programs, and they usually were part of horizontal rather than vertical unions *(stopansko obedinenie)*.

Between 1981 and 1988, through a special program, some 400 to 500 small- to medium-sized enterprises (SMEs) were founded and equipped with state-of-the-art technology, imported mostly from Western countries. In January 1989, the right of citizens to set up a firm was established and regulated. By the end of that year 9,583 private firms had been registered, including 7,875 sole proprietorships, 1,592 collectives and 116 limited-liabilty companies.

But the rapid development of small business really began after 1990. In the five years since then, the number of small enterprises has increased tremendously.

This increase was due to several factors. As state enterprises were decentralized, their number grew from 597 to 19,287, with about 12,000 of them being classified as SMEs. The number of other non-private firms — cooperative, municipal and others — also increased. By the end of 1994 there were 25,798 of these, at least half of them SMEs.

The number of small private enterprises grew fastest of all. As of December 31, 1994 there were 412,562 private firms in Bulgaria, practically all of them small. Only 0.2 per cent — or about 1,000 — had more than 50 employees. Altogether Bulgaria currently has more than 420,000 small enterprises, employing more than 1 million people.

The revival of small business can be tied directly to the revival of private business — not only because 96 per cent to 97 per cent of the small enterprises are private, but because their creation reflects the revival of entrepreneurship in Bulgaria.

In analyzing the activities of small enterprises in Bulgaria, it should be noted that statistical data exists for only about 70 per cent of them. The reasons for this include failure or refusal to release information, incorrect address registration, firms going out of business without legal notice, etc. This limited data on small business is an additional reason for conducting economic and sociological research in the field.

Small businesses are concentrated mostly in the trade sector: about 60 per cent of the total. Significantly smaller shares — from 5 per cent to 10 per cent of the total — are in the manufacturing, transportation, and construction sectors.

The small-business size structure is of great interest. About 90 per cent of the businesses have fewer than five employees. The percentage is highest in trade and transportation, and relatively lower in manufacturing and construction.

Data on size structure in a transition economy could be analyzed more precisely if compared with the same data in developed countries. This method is highly conditional, but if we take for example the manufacturing sector, the range of differences among the developed countries is not great, and for each country the total number of businesses as well as the size distribution are relatively stable. That is why we believe that data for small West European countries, adjusted to the population of Bulgaria, would give us a general idea of possible trends in small-business size structure in Bulgaria.

If we make comparisons with these data, we find first that the total number of businesses in Bulgaria with six to 50 employees is smaller than the number of such businesses in the developed countries. Second, we find that the number of Bulgarian businesses with 21 to 50 employees is insufficient.

The analysis of SME size structure indirectly supports the conclusion that entrepreneurship in Bulgaria is primarily entrepreneurship in general, with frequent changes in the subject of business activity. Comparison with developed countries shows that further small business development can increase the number of enterprises with 6 to 50 employees. This corroborates the importance of establishing consulting centers to support the creation and development of small businesses with predetermined and well-defined objectives.

**The ESBID Study of Entrepreneurship
and Small Business:
Some Preliminary Results**

ESBID (Entrepreneurship and Small Business Development in Bulgaria 1993-1996) is a research project created to study both the theoretical and practical aspects of the creation and development of SMEs in Bulgaria's private sector. Purposes of the project include:

1   analysis of the role of small business in the economic and industrial structure of the country and its contribution to the formation of a so-called 'dual economy,' taking into account features specific to Bulgaria.

2   analysis of key factors in the business environment that support (or do not support) small-business development: government regulations, markets, resources, available technologies, and social/cultural characteristics including entrepreneurial traditions.

3   analysis of opportunities and problems in the starup of SMEs, including the role of the business plan in effective planning and control of resources.

4   analysis of opportunities and problems in the management and development of newly established SMEs.

The project is financed wholly by Bulgarian sources — foundations and private firms — as the results will be used in education, research and management by governmental, private and public institutions.

Purposes 2, 3 and 4 will be achieved basically through the study of about 120 SMEs. The EFER questionnaire (developed by the European Foundation for Entrepreneurship Research, and already implemented in some CEE countries) is being used, complemented with Bulgarian-specific questions. A distinctive feature of this method is that it makes it possible to identify the so-called 'dynamic entrepreneurs' who are growth-oriented, use highly productive equipment, and play the role of drivers in the economy. After such entrepreneurs are found, some case studies will be conducted to give a more complete and in-depth picture of the processes involved.

So far, responses to the questionnare have been received from some of the firms. On the basis of 41 of these firms — all from Haskovo Province, in southern Bulgaria — we will present some preliminary findings, and try to connect them with other available information in order to make useful comparisons and draw some tentative conclusions.

From Table 1, General Profile of SMEs, we can paint a general picture of the firms covered in the study. Their differentiation as to legal form is about as expected, with a prevalence of sole proprietorships. The dominance of this form is easily explained by small entrepreneurial traditions, a shortage of capital, and hard macroeconomics conditions for business.

The greater experience of manufacturing firms (listed under 'production' in Table 1) is probably due to former managers and specialists continuing their profession by turning to private entrepreneurship.

The general impression is that the typical microfirm prevails in Haskovo Province, despite the lack of complete information on some business sectors.

Table 1:
General profile of SMEs

Main field of activity

Characteristics	Production	Trade	Construction	Services and others	Total*
	44.0 %	34.0 %	14.6 %	7.4 %	100.0 %
Legal status					
Sole proprietorship	26.9 %	19.3 %	2.4 %	7.4 %	56.0 %
Partnership	9.8 %	4.9 %	4.9 %	-	19.6 %
Limited liability company	2.4 %	9.8 %	7.3 %	-	19.5 %
Joint stock company	4.9 %	-	-	-	4.9 %
Years of existence					
Less than one	4.9 %	9.7 %	2.4 %	2.5 %	19.5 %
from 1 to 2	9.8 %	7.3 %	-	4.9 %	22.0 %
3 and longer	29.3 %	17.0 %	12.2 %		58.5 %
Number of employees					
one-person firms	-	2.4 %	-	4.9 %	7.3 %
from 2 to 10	19.5 %	23.3 %	-	2.5 %	45.3 %
from 11 to 30	9.8 %	7.3 %	7.3 %	-	24.4 %
from 31 to 50	9.8 %	-	-	-	9.8 %
51 and more	4.9 %	-	7.3 %	-	12.2 %

* Percentages are rounded to make totals add up to 100% for each group of characteristics.

64

Profile of the entrepreneurs

From Table 2, Profile by Age and Gender, we see that most entrepreneurs are men. This corresponds with data for the country as a whole (EIM, 1992). The female entrepreneurs younger than 25 are noteworthy; one hypothesis is they are heiresses of existing entrepreneurs. The age distribution generally conforms to previous studies, with the dominant age between 36 and 45.

Table 2:
Profile by age and gender

Age	*Gender*		
	Male	**Female**	**Total**
To 25 years	-	4.9 %	4.9 %
From 26 to 35	24.4 %	-	24.4 %
From 36 to 45	36.6 %	9.8 %	46.4 %
From 46 to 55	19.5 %	2.4 %	21.9%
Over 55	2.4 %	-	2.4 %
Total	82.9 %	17.1 %	100.0 %

Most of the entrepreneurs have technical educations (see Table 3, Education and Pre-Startup Experience of Entrepreneurs). This corresponds with the fact that most specialists and managers in state-owned enterprises had technical educations, and some of them moved into SMEs.

An exceptionally large share of the entrepreneurs — more than half — have higher education degrees. At the same time, a significant number have relatively little work experience. An interesting comparison can be made here to West European entrepreneurs, whose situation is the reverse: they tend to have relatively less education and more experience. In our opinion this is natural, given the existing long market traditions in West Europe and the supporting infrastructure to assist entrepreneurs with lower education levels. It also seems logical that the opposite would be true of entrepreneurs in Bulgaria, where people who are highly educated might have a better chance to succeed in one unique transition.

Table 3:
Education and Pre-Startup Experience of Entrepreneurs

Educational degree	Type of education			Experience			
	Technical	Economic	Other	1 to 3 yrs	3 to 10 yrs	over 10 yrs	Total
High school	36.6%	4.9%	2.4%	14.6%	2.4%	26.9%	43.9%
University	24.4%	14.6%	9.8%	9.8%	12.2%	26.8%	48.8%
Post-graduate	7.3%	-	-	-	4.9%	2.4%	7.3%
Total	68.3%	19.5%	12.2%	24.4%	19.5%	56.1%	100.0%

In Table 4, Motivations of Entrepreneurs, the most interesting result is that — contrary to our initial hypothesis — the most common main motive for starting a firm is not 'economic necessity,' but 'independence.' This motive correlates strongly with the respective practical reason, 'few job opportunities outside private sector.' In comparison, the percentage who cited 'economic necessity/lost job' is not so high. It must be considered that Haskovo Province has a relatively low unemployment rate. Yet indirectly, the other reasons can also be interpreted as economic, so that for all practical purposes we can speak of so-called 'forced entrepreneurship' occurring here.

Also noteworthy are the small number who cited 'career/security' or 'status/prestige' as motives. This is explainable if one keeps in mind: (a) the transitional condition of the country and the insecurity attending this transition; and (b) the relatively conservative — but realistic — disposition of the region's inhabitants despite the high education levels.

All of this indirectly corroborates the thesis of number of researchers (for example Drucker, 1985) that entrepreneurship is more a social-psychological than economic phenomenon.

Table 4:
Motivations of entrepreneurs

Primary reason for starting business	Main motive							Total
	1	2	3	4	5	6	7	
Lost job	4.9%	-	-	14.6%	-	-	-	24.4%
Frustrated with work in state-owned enterprise	2.4%	9.8%	-	4.9%	-	2.4%	2.4%	21.9%
Few job opportunities outside private sector	-	19.5%	-	-	2.4%	2.4%	2.4%	26.7%
Unsatisfied with salary	-	-	-	2.4%	-	-	-	2.4%
Having profitable idea	2.4%	12.2%	4.9%	-	-	-	-	19.5%
Other	-	2.4%	-	-	-	-	2.4%	4.8%
Total	9.8%	48.8%	4.9%	21.9%	2.4%	4.8 %	7.3%	100.0 %

Motive
Legend: 1 *Achievement (self-expression)*   5 *Career/security*
            2 *Independence*   6 *Status/prestige*
            3 *More money*   7 *Other*
            4 *Economic necessity*

Starting Up

The biggest problem facing any entrepreneur is financing, especially in the very beginning. The restrictive monetary policy prevents the granting of long-term investment loans. Also the lack of reliable business projections and a well-prepared business plan discourages potential investors. Thus most entrepreneurs had started with insufficient capital compared to their needs.

Nevertheless Table 5, Sources of Financing, shows that 37.5 per cent of the entrepreneurs surveyed in Haskovo Province were able to obtain bank loans for starting their businesses. This is surprising compared to figures for the rest of Bulgaria and other CEE nations, which show between 3 per cent and 5 per cent of entrepreneurs using bank loans. One possible explanation may be the small amount of borrowed capital needed by entrepreneurs.

Table 5:
Sources of Financing When Starting a Business

Owners' savings	40 %
Borrowing from family/friends	2.5 %
Supplier credits	12.5 %
Buyer credits	7.5 %
Bank loan	37.5 %
Total	100 %

Management

Table 6 shows the correlation between the legal form of the business and participation in the firm's management; it shows that in most firms, only the owners manage. Factors limiting the size and extent of management are the small size of the firms (in terms of sheer number of staff), as well as reluctance of the owners to share what we call their 'home kitchen secrets.' A detailed study of the questionnaire shows that very few owners would share management with their partners even if this were to give them additional benefits. There is little sharing of management participation even in limited-liability companies. Reasons for this are the presence of one-owner limited-liability companies on the one hand, and a desire for unity of decision-making on the other.

Table 6:
Firm management

Legal form

Who manages the business?	Sole proprietor-ship	Partner-ship	Limited liability company	Joint stock company	Total
Only the owner	39.1 %	7.3 %	12.2 %	-	58.6%
Management team of owners	7.3 %	4.9 %	4.9 %	-	17.1%
Management team of owners and non-owners	9.8 %	7.3 %	2.4 %	4.8 %	24.3 %
Management team of non-owners					
Total	56.2 %	19.5 %	19.5 %	4.8 %	100 %

For Table 7, Factors Affecting the Business, each entrepreneur was asked to cite the main problem and the main reason for success of the business. Generally the responses confirm findings from other studies (such as EIM-1992). The news here is the considerable percentage of firms having difficulties collecting payments. Undoubtedly this is due to complicated economic situation in the country — high inflation, fluctuations of the currency exchange rate, etc. — which worsens the economic condition of SMEs, especially the smallest ones.

Under 'main reason for success,' a significant number cited the building of good relationships, especially with clients. The interesting thing here, given the high education level of enterpreneurs, is that few considered education an important factor. This may be due to the general fact that 'You don't know how important something is unless you don't have it,' and also to the belief that in doing business, social connections take first place.

It seems most significant that hardly anyone felt a pressing need for new technology, or cited innovation as a reason for success. Undoubtedly there are many reasons for this: the small size of the firms and their limited resources, the risk and difficulty of getting a return on investment, the fact that most are operating in traditional lines of business, and (at present) the lack of a long-term strategy for the business.

Table 7:
Factors Affecting the Business

	Production 44.0 %	Trade 34.0 %	Others 22.0 %	Total 100.0 %
The main problem affecting the business				
Insufficient financial strength / inability to obtain financing	17.0 %	17.0 %	4.9 %	38.9 %
Difficulties in collecting payments	4.9 %	4.9 %	2.4 %	12.2 %
Unfavorable governmental regulation	4.9 %	-	-	4.9 %
Insufficient market	4.5 %	7.3 %	12.2 %	24.0 %
Limited availability of skilled workers	-	2.4 %	-	2.4 %
Out-of-date technology	2.4 %	-	2.4 %	4.8 %
The main reason for success of the business				
Good relations with customers/clients	2.4 %	17 %	4.9 %	24.3 %
Product/service quality	4.9 %	2.4 %	-	7.3 %
Experience of the owner/management team	14.6 %	4.9 %	7.3 %	26.8 %
Connections	-	4.9 %	-	4.9 %
Marketing of product/service	7.3 %	-	2.4 %	9.7 %
Education of the owner/management team	7.3 %	2.4 %	2.4 %	12.1 %
Adequate financing	2.4 %	-	-	2.4 %
Innovations	2.4 %	-	-	2.4 %

At first glance Table 8, The Most Useful Training for Entrepreneurs, seems to contradict Table 7. But if we ignore Table 7's 'relations with customers/clients' and 'connections' — which defy training — then things fall into place. Marketing (including the perception of quality), financing, and general management know-how rank high in both tables. The importance assigned to 'import/export' training probably implies intentions to internationalize the business.

Table 8:
Most Useful Training for Entrepreneurs

Training courses	Frequency cited *
Marketing	29.3 %
How to obtain financing	17.1 %
Management	17.1 %
Languages	17.0 %
Import/export	17.0 %
Technical/technology	14.6 %
Accounting (bookkeeping)	9.8 %
Legal	2.4 %
None	9.8 %

* Figures add up to more than 100% because some respondents gave more than one answer.

Business environment

For Table 9, entrepreneurs were asked to evaluate the impact of factors in the business environment. The prevalance of positive responses to business registration procedures is impressive — especially considering that the old system, which existed until recently, was notoriously bureaucratic.

The negative ratings given to credit access and terms are not surprising. As in other studies, the biggest problem here is the high interest rates, which are murderous for most SMEs, especially in manufacturing. Only trading firms that use short-term credits are favored to a certain extent.

The highly negative responses to the tax system — and to the government's attitude toward small business — present a worrisome picture. What we see here may be an effect of the value-added tax, which was recently implemented without much preparation or warning.

It is pleasing to see a high percentage feeling positive about the public's attitude toward small private business. Regional factors may come into play here, due to the existence of entrepreneurial traditions in Haskovo Province.

Table 9:
Business Environment — Evaluation by Entrepreneurs

Characteristic of the environment	Entrepreneurs' evaluation			
	Very Negative	Negative	Neutral	Positive
Registration of businesses	-	12.2 %	39.0 %	48.8 %
Financing and credit:				
- access to credit	-	30.0 %	n.a.	n.a.
- interest rate	-	55.0 %	n.a.	n.a.
- credit conditions and terms	-	35.0 %	n.a.	n.a.
Impact of taxes:				
- on the rate of profitability	-	95.1 %	4.9 %	
- on the reinvesting of profit	-	63.4 %	7.3 %	29.3 %
- on starting a business	-	65.9 %	26.8 %	7.3 %
Attitude of the government	34.1 %	31.7 %	24.4 %	9.8 %
Attitude of the people	-	17.0 %	36.6 %	46.4 %

Conclusions

The results of the ESBID project presented in this paper, although preliminary and incomplete, can be pieced together to give us a rough mosaic of small business in Bulgaria. On the dark side of the picture are the barriers to business creation and development: high taxes, a lack of significant preferences, difficulty of access to credit (especially high interest rates), and a lack of institutional support for SMEs. On the other side can be seen the lights at the end of the tunnel, such as the relative absence of bureaucratic obstacles to starting a business, the relatively significant number of entrepreneurs having intentions to invest, and a change for the better in people's attitude toward entrepreneurial activity.

Further research will help to fill in the mosaic — and to rearrange it. Despite its disadvantages, a study like the ESBID project can be used not only to benchmark and analyze the present, but to shape decisions about the future of SMEs in Bulgaria.

Part Three
CASE STUDIES ON SBDCs

8 Gdynia SBDC: Operations in 1994

Przemyslaw Kulawczuk
Director, Gdynia/Gdansk Center,
Polish-American Small Business Advisory Foundation

1994 was a very important year for the Polish-American Small Business Development Center in Gdynia/Gdansk. The project underwent considerable transformation in adjusting to the economic environment of the Gdansk Seaside region. Major changes included gaining a new local partner, moving into new premises in Gdynia, revision of the marketing strategy for the Center, and revision of the service strategy to provide more impact. These efforts made it possible to achieve better results.

Geographic notes: 'Gdansk Seaside' is the common name for Eastern Pomerania, a region on the Baltic coast extending about 120 km to the west of Gdansk, 70 km to the east, and about 120 km inland. The Tricity (or Tricities) referred to in this paper is a single metropolitan area with three independent cities: Gdansk, Gdynia, and Sopot.

Gaining a New Local Partner

The decision to locate a Polish-American small business advisory center in this region was based on two factors. The first was the high level of new business creation in the Seaside region. The second was the possibility of achieving visible and rapid effects, to prove the efficacy of adapting the American SBDC model to Polish conditions.

Following the American model, the Center was initially located in 1992 on the premises of one of the Tricities' colleges, the Technical University of Gdansk. Having the Technical University as a host contributed greatly to the creation of a professional image for the Center, and the facilities were good. This arrangement enabled the Center to give advisory assistance to a large number of clients: In the first year, 478 took part in individual counseling sessions and 1611 in seminars and courses.

As time went on, the immense initial demand tended to slow down. By 1994 it was evident the Center would have to concentrate on more complex work with a smaller group of clients. The situation also demanded a more client–oriented approach, which meant going out looking for entrepreneurs who needed help. The Center's image was to be reconstructed from that of para-academic institution, coexisting with a college, to that of a professional business consulting center, easily accessible to clients.

It was decided that aligning the Center with the local government of one of the Tricities would help make this possible. Presumably the goals of the local government would be congruent with those of the Polish–American project, because they shared a concern for the economic growth of the region, especially in the private sector.

After talks with local government authorities, the City of Gdynia was chosen to be strategic partner of the project in the Seaside region. Its public officials were very dynamic in supporting business activities. Gdynia had launched a World Trade Center project, and was a host of the internationally-important small business meeting 'Europartenariat 1994.' The city also was characterized by a good economic infrastructure.

Thus the Polish–American Foundation turned to the City of Gdynia with a proposal to establish a new mutual undertaking: the Gdynia Polish–American Small Business Development Center. Thanks to assistance from City authorities — Mrs. Mayor Franciszka Cegielska, Deputy Mayor Maciej Brzeski, and the city executive team — the president of Polish Chamber of Commerce, Dr. Andrzej Arendarski, signed a cooperation agreement with Gdynia on May 17,1994.

City authorities offered premises of 94 square meters [about 1,000 square feet] and became patrons of the project. After necessary renovations, the Gdynia SBDC was inaugurated on August 3. Cooperation with city authorities produced an increase in counseled clients from about 30 to 40 per month in early 1994 to about 60 per month in the latter part of the year. At the same time, the percentage of clients who were startups (as distinct from ongoing businesses) increased from 30 per cent in the first quarter of 1994 to 42 per cent in the last quarter.

Revision of Marketing Strategy

Changing the Center's location required complex promotional activities. The aim was to make access to the Center easier for new clients from the northern part of the metropolitan area, while maintaining ties with clients from the southern part of the Tricities (especially Gdansk).

The new promotion strategy was based on careful study of the approaches taken by two business concerns, Coca-Cola Poland and Masterfood Poland.

Considerable stress was placed on fixed advertising elements, such as billboards and placards, promotional items, and in-company and in-store displays. A big advantage of these is that once made and installed, they are inexpensive or even cost–free to use. Fixed elements also create the impression of a constant presence among customers and growing demand for the products or services offered.

Advertising, information and direction boards for the Polish-American project were installed at seven key points in Gdynia, including City Hall, Pomorski Credit Bank, the Chamber of Commerce, and in three of the more popular stores of the main shopping district on Swietojanska Street. Also, Gdynia's business-activity registration bodies directed many new entrepreneurs to the Center by handing out supplied leaflets. These factors generated increased demand for counseling.

Impact on the Private-Sector Infrastructure

Although the main task of the Center is to advise small businesses, its strategic mission was expanded in 1994. The Center's staff began efforts to help improve the infrastructure of service and support for the private business sector — starting with banks and local authorities.

As experience has shown, one of the chief barriers to small business growth is the shortage of financial resources. In Poland, especially serious problems could be found in the area of bank loans, as loan officers and their sales techniques were not attuned to the needs of small companies. So the Gdynia/Gdansk Center developed a cooperative project with the Gdansk Banking Academy, titled 'The improvement of Credit Lines to SMEs.' Consultants from the Center's staff helped to gather and analyze opinions of small-company clients on banking procedures and credit barriers. The consultants also delivered a report on ways of helping small entrepreneurs to prepare credit documents, and introduced foreign experiences in the field of small-business credit problems. In cooperation with Gdansk Banking Academy employees, a report on improving loan procedures for small enterprises was worked out.

One part of this report contained proposals for increasing the sales of bank loans to SMEs. Since the Center's team had extensive knowledge of sales techniques, the consultants developed a training project for loan officers. Through a fruitful cooperation with Bank Gdanski, a formal training was arranged for that bank's credit inspectors. The first course took place in November 1994. It was highly appreciated by the participants. Bank Gdanski authorities were deeply satisfied as well, and scheduled a series of similar sessions to be organized by the Gdynia SBDC in 1995. Loan officers from 18 local branches of the bank are to be trained regularly. The Center hopes this will broaden the prospects for small business loans at Bank Gdanski, the seventh largest in Poland in terms of assets.

Together with the Institute for Private Enterprise and Democracy, associated with the Polish Chamber of Commerce, the Center undertook another major project. This one had to do with enterprise and investment in rural areas. The Center's staff participated in writing a report titled 'The Development of Rural Communities,' which described practical means of promoting new economic enterprises in these communities. More than 1,000 copies of the report were printed. It was welcomed with great interest by local authorities in rural areas, who ordered numerous copies. Right now, the Center is preparing a training program for local authorities, on ways of supporting new investments.

Experience shows that working to build the business support structure has some unquestioned advantages. It lays the patterns for an overall 'culture' of modern small business support. It is also a method of service delivery with low unit costs. The results are concrete and fruitful.

Cooperation with Local Partners

While one of the Center's strategic changes was to try to impact the support infrastructure, the other was to establish stronger ties with local partners.

Acquiring the City of Gdynia as a partner was, of course, a major step. It gave the Center substantial and convenient premises, close to the downtown district, in which to do profitable counseling. Furthermore, City Council invited the Center's director to participate in the work of Gdynia's Commission on Finance and Strategy Development. The director lends his knowledge and experience to assist city authorities in major strategic undertakings.

A close relationship with the government of Gdynia helps the Center provide a wide spectrum of counseling services to the city's small businesses. The Center also contributes to the image of Gdynia as a supporter of new economic enterprises. Its participation in Europartenariat '94 and in the Gdansk Television program 'Americans in Gdynia,' and a series of articles in the local periodicals *Gdynia Courier* and *City Hall* are examples of this.

The Center also cooperates with the Economic and Trade Chamber. Consultants from the Center helped to start a training program for members of the Chamber.

Selected Results of Advisory
and Training Activities in 1994

- With the help of a legal consultant from the Center, the Dusted & Dusted company of Gdansk, a supplier of bathroom fixtures, managed to withdraw from a disadvantageous contract for commercial space rental. Subsequently the company signed a new contract on much better terms.

- Tan Viet, an export–import company in Gdansk, used the aid of a credit consultant to obtain an import loan. The loan enabled the company to substantially increase sales.

- The Gogra company of Gdynia, a supplier of single–use tableware for restaurants, worked with a marketing consultant to design layouts of business letters to clients. This helped to increase output and create two workplaces.

- The furniture cooperative Dab of Gdynia prepared its first marketing plan and promotion strategy with the help of a marketing consultant. A new appreciation of the importance of these issues led the company to establish a specialized Marketing and Sales Department.

- Insurance agent Krzysztof Witulski used techniques learned from a sales specialist to create a mail campaign aimed at gaining new life-insurance clients.

- The Drobpol company of Zukowo approached the Foundation for assistance with sales problems. Its employees were inexperienced at selling and sales had declined. After the Foundation trained three members of Drobpol's sales staff, quality of client service improved, as did the firm's financial condition.

- The owner of Robert's Tourist Equipment, Roman Werdon, enrolled in a marketing course at the Center. He then took part in several consulting sessions and prepared a business plan and loan application. Werdon was granted a loan to increase production of mountaineering sleeping bags for export.

9 Moving to Sustainability in Lódz

Izabela Firkowska
Director
Small Business Advisory Center, Lódz
Polish-American Small Business Advisory Foundation

Introduction

Systemic turnaround in Poland at the end of 1980s resulted in changes to the ownership structures in the economy. The large state-owned enterprises which hitherto had prevailed turned out to be hardly flexible in adjusting to the new reality, in which the economy began to be market-driven.

The gap that emerged was filled by small enterprises which were very responsive to the demands, grew dynamically, and were capable of swift adjustment to changing conditions.

Buoyant growth of small to medium-sized enterprises stemmed from an easily achieved penetration of market niches in sectors such as commerce, services, building and construction, and some segments of the market for transport services. The majority of the new enterprises were small. Currently private firms employing up to five people account for 93 per cent of all the businesses active in Poland.

However, structural changes in the Polish private sector are not positive. The sector is characterized by considerable dilution, low capitalization, a small share of limited-liability and joint-stock companies, and decidedly too small a presence in industry. Moreover, knowledge of the principles and rules of running a business in a market economy is not sufficient to enable entrepreneurs to function efficiently and thus stay in the market. These problems constitute a barrier to further growth of the private sector in Poland. The situation requires an immense effort to make economic education and data, as well as consulting and advisory services, available even to the smallest of the enterprises.

The Role of the Foundation

Small and medium-sized enterprises need support for several reasons. They tend to be started by people whose experience and skills are totally different from what is required to run one's own business. Also, the scarcity of Polish capital makes Polish companies economize on expenditures for marketing, financial, tax and legal advisory services. Instead of starting from a business plan, they follow the principle of the 'lucky draw,' which increases the likelihood of failure.

These are the challenges being acted upon by the Polish-American Advisory Foundation. Through its Centers in Lódz and other cities, it offers guidance to entrepreneurs on how to set up operations and verify the concept of the business. The principal objective of the Foundation is to impart professional knowledge to those who start businesses with limited ability to pay for advisory services. Another key objective is to propagate among entrepreneurs an awareness of the need for ongoing, systematic learning, if they are to manage their businesses effectively.

Service to companies which already have been established, and now need advice to support further growth and ensure survival, should be structured in a somewhat different way. In such cases, the role of the Center would entail continuous cooperation with a company. Thereby the Center would help these businesses to run more efficiently and effectively, avoiding erroneous decisions and haphazard action. Training in selected aspects of marketing, business administration and management as well as negotiation and foreign trade will be very helpful to such enterprises. This training should be provided by recognized specialists who have both theoretical knowledge and practical experience in the subjects concerned.

Sustainability and Quality

The need for an institution to support small business is justified by the increase in the number of small companies which must overcome considerable difficulties to strengthen their market position. Left to fend for themselves, they cannot effectively solve problems and may fail.

Growth of the small business sector is pivotal for the economic growth of the region and the success of policies aimed at reducing unemployment. It acquired particular significance in the Lódz region, where unemployment rates surged drastically after the collapse of the large state-owned cotton mills. In Lódz — a city of some 800,000 inhabitants — over 100,000 occupationally active people are jobless, many of them young and dynamic individuals below the age of 40. With few job openings, starting a business of one's own emerges as the only means to survive for many. But given the growing competitiveness of the market environment, the lack of knowledge and business experience and the shortage of startup capital can prove to be serious hindrances.

A shrinkage in further growth of small and medium-sized businesses, due to the weakness of this sector, indicates an urgent need to support the development of small companies.

The sustainability of this particular Small Business Development Center is a function of the demand of business owners for the services provided by the Center. Sustainability also is a function of how useful and effective these services are perceived to be.

During the Center's two years of operation, we have managed to prove that we are needed. As data below will indicate, our advisory and training assistance has been fully accepted by local authorities and by the business community — including other institutions supporting small business development.

For instance, the concept of helping small and medium-sized businesses has been recognized in banking circles. Our Center's cooperation with the Polish-American Enterprise Fund in Lódz, Bank Przemyslowo Handlowy, and Powszechny Bank Gospodarczy has been fruitful. The Banks and the Center have exchanged information and assistance, with especially visible results in the area of helping companies apply for loans. Bank officers have responded very positively to business plans developed in conjunction with the Center. In their opinion, loan officers cannot be so comprehensively and deeply involved in business projects submitted to them.

Perhaps the most crucial feedback has come from clients of the Center, who positively evaluate the assistance they receive. To date, 849 clients have taken advantage of our advisory services, and training sessions have been attended by 2,018 people. We proved to be very useful to these clients, according to questionnaires adminstered by the Foundation. A considerable number of those who expressed favorable responses are very influential opinion-makers in the community.

Supporting business and counteracting unemployment are the main goals of local government in the Lódz region. The concept of providing assistance to small businesses is not new to the local authorities here, yet it is difficult to obtain funding from them for the Center, as financial aid is also sought by a number of similar projects, and funds are limited. Assistance to projects of a larger scale than those in which the Center is involved seems a more likely alternative. In the near future, projects to create an entrepreneurship incubator and a Credit Guarantee Fund will be considered.

To sum up, the Center's sustainability depends on its ability to provide big usefulness to the small business community. Usefulness should be assessed by the degree to which the needs of the Center's clients are satisfied, and tested in light of the quality of advisory and training services provided.

Quality standards lead to implementation of the following criteria, which should guide ongoing activity at the Center as well as shape the direction of future activities:

- careful selection of consultants and lecturers

- high professional and content standards for consulting and training

- excellent customer service and efficient organization

- efficiency in deployment of funds

- appropriate identification of problems signaled to the Center by customers

- upgrading staff skills

- development of the Center's image

- co-operation with the business community.

Revenue Generation

Since we are approaching the end of the third year in which funding to the Advisory Centers has been provided by the US Congress, the question of how the Foundation's activities will be financed in the near future is asked more frequently. We recognize that survival depends on sourcing funds to fulfill the objectives set forth in the Foundation's charter. The fact that the usefulness of our Center has been proved convinces us that it is worth making an effort to secure such funding.

The current situation is very difficult. This means that management of the Centers need to be considerably involved in raising funds. Having reviewed potential fund providers we may identify the following solutions:

- obtaining subsidies from local authorities

- applying for grants to foreign fund providers

- self-financing

The likelihood of funding from local authorities depends on evaluation of the extent to which the Center contributes to local entrepreneurship. It should be emphasized that local authorities are not keen on financing the entire operations of the Center, owing to the scarcity of resources.

Securing office premises from local authorities is the strongest possibility here. Another form of financing that may be offered is to vest the Center with implementation of various projects and training initiatives sponsored by local authorities. (For example, the Center could handle a training program for unemployed people who intend to start their own businesses.)

Foreign aid also is possible. The Lódz Center already has applied to the STRUDER program for funds to offer training courses and advisory services to small importers and exporters, and to publish a foreign-trade textbook for them. There is a likelihood the funds will be obtained.

Self-financing will involve provision of training and courses on a commercial basis. Our first successful efforts in this regard allow us to expect that this, too, will be an appropriate source of funding for the Center.

Networking and Marketing

The Foundation works with the media to a significant extent. Directors of the Center have been interviewed frequently by print journalists as well as taking part in radio and TV programs. Journalists have shown immense goodwill to the Center and its staff.

The Center cooperates closely with many organizations whose goals include education, training, and helping small enterprises. The following deserve a mention in this context: the Foundation for Social and Economic Initiatives, *Solidarnocz* Economic Foundation, Gdansk Academy of Banking, the US Peace Corps, Job Centers, the Polish Union of the Unemployed, Economic Chambers, the Department of Employment at the Ministry of Labor and Social Policy, the Foundation for Rural Area Water Supply, Polish-American Entrepreneurship Clubs and many others. Exchanges of information with such groups, often accompanied by joint efforts, allow the needs of small enterprises to be met more effectively.

Two Examples of Partnership

In 1994, for example, the Lódz SBAC cooperated with two institutions involved in developing enterpreneurship: the Economic Promotion and Services to Foreigners Desk at City Council, and the Lódz branch of the Polish Economic Chamber.

We exchanged information with the Desk on 'matchmaking' opportunities for potential business partners, both domestic and foreign. All needs of the

Center's clients in the areas of business cooperation, identification of market outlets, or suppliers were entered in a computer database at the Desk. Managers of the Center also were invited to business events in the city, to establish new contacts and further promote the Center's activities.

Last year alone the Desk lodged about 20 applications for help in building links with domestic and foreign business partners. One result was the signing of a significant contract for children's clothing between our client — a family-owned clothing manufacturer — and a German business. This helped the Company expand its market outlets and already has yielded two new jobs.

In the middle of 1994 we cooperated intensively with the Polish Economic Chamber/Lódz Branch, which emerged from its predecessor, the Lódz office of the Polish Chamber of Foreign Trade.

The evolution and importance of the Chamber should be noted here. In the command economy, when foreign trade was reserved to the State, there were a number of dynamic Foreign Trade Offices in Lódz that maintained regular ties with the Chamber. Currently, after the systemic turnaround, the Chamber works with a number of private companies involved in foreign trade, while maintaining relationships with large state-owned (and currently privatized) firms active in international markets. And recently a new group — the Exporters' and Importers' Club — was established within the framework of the Chamber.

All of the above obviously attracted the Center's interest. It was in full accord with the specialty receiving priority in the Center, foreign trade. Interest in this issue had been stimulated by our clients, who indicated they had numerous problems in connection with it.

In 1994 the Center held six training courses and seminars on foreign trade on the premises of the Chamber. The managers of the Chamber actively helped in promoting the seminars and canvassing. The Chamber's contacts with businesses and the Exporters' and Importers' Club were of particular value.

It should be stressed that the promotional efforts of the Foundation are primarily through free channels, such as media coverage generated by interviews, press releases, and seminars or other events that attract the media. Also, many companies have learned about the Foundation by word of mouth, from previous clients.

10 Warsaw SBAC: Activities in 1994

Andrzej Stasiek, PhD
Director
Small Business Advisory Center, Warsaw
Polish-American Small Business Advisory Foundation

The Year in Review

In 1994 the Warsaw Center enjoyed a good reputation in the small business community. Because of our consultants' experience and high standards of performance, the Center team decided to focus on a specific group of clients. We targeted clients with significant economic potential, oriented for development and looking for advisory assistance on a continuing basis.

This shift in strategy was facilitated by a change in location. The Warsaw Center moved to the Polish Chamber of Commerce building, bringing it closer to entrepreneurs seeking help, both Polish and foreign. (An example of work with foreign partners was cooperation with one of the Italian local economic chambers, which resulted in preparation of a 'Business Guide.')

The Center also developed contacts with local financial institutions, offering help in the evaluation of projects. Through relationships with the Main School of Commerce — particularly its College of Business Administration — the Center can access high-quality assistance as needed.

In 1994 the Center turned to the Foundation for help in building cooperation with Poland's Ministry of Privatization. As a result of these efforts, some of the most highly regarded entrepreneurial firms in Poland began to use the counseling services of the Warsaw Center. Two examples are United Publishers, a partner of Pepsico–Poland; and Vispol, a major dealer of trucks through a leasing system.

Services for Private Firms

From the opening of the Warsaw Center until today (March 1, 1995), advisory help has been provided to nearly 800 clients. Every day new clients come, looking for economic or marketing advice, checking their chances of getting a bank loan. The main problem of existing small businesses is adjusting to the changing economic and financial environment in Poland. Owners often ask for help in reorganizing their companies structurally and operationally. They also struggle with managerial problems.

It is impossible to meet the great demand for counseling. Clients' high expectations sometimes exceed what the Center can offer. The Center's staff has drawn the following conclusions:

- There is a group of problems that cannot be solved by the Center's consultants, because of personnel and financial limitations. Foremost among these are questions of promotion and marketing abroad, and help in seeking foreign partners.

- The Center's mission is to assist clients in handling their problems. This means the client must cooperate, instead of passively waiting for the outcome. A consultant should be able to recognize the necessary level of his involvement. This rule also serves the goal of educating Polish entrepreneurs.

- A consultant is not always able to get at the core of the issue. Clients often have problems articulating their problems.

- Outcomes of consulting are not always immediate. There are problems that need a long–term approach, such as preparing credit documentation.

- Sometimes a client does not agree with a solution suggested by a consultant. An example would be questions of financing, when loan terms (such as interest rates, credit securities and terms of payment) are not acceptable to a particular businessman.

Cooperation with Banks and the Media

From the beginning, the Warsaw Center adopted a principle of cooperation with local financial institutions and mass media. For example:

PKO BP Rotunda is a bank with which the Center launched joint efforts in 1994. A series of articles titled 'In Defense of the Zloty' was published in local periodicals and broadcast on the radio. Consultants presented a bank loan offer given by the bank to entrepreneurs, and discussed the costs of credit granted in domestic currency. They also tried to introduce a new, more client–oriented image of PKO BP. Along with these promotional activities, the Center began organizing a training program on loan and marketing analysis attuned to small business needs. It is designed for the bank's credit representatives and inspectors.

The Polish–American Enterprise Fund in Warsaw is another partner of the Warsaw SBAC. In November 1994 the Fund opened the Enterprise Corporation, the main purpose of which is small enterprise support through a loan program. Profitability, good financial standing and credibility, along with financial forecasts for new projects, are the principal criteria for granting loans by the Corporation. The Center's task is to perform a preliminary financial evaluation of clients' proposals. After completing and discussing credit applications and accompanying documents, the client is directed to a loan officer. In order to work with the Enterprise Corporation, the Center's consultants were trained in the use of the necessary forms.

Economic Union Bank is an incorporated company of cooperative banks located in Central and Eastern Poland. It specializes in credit for agriculture and the food industry. Currently it is working to widen its offerings; the Center was invited to cooperate in the promotion of new activities. The Center's consultants also advise potential clients of the Bank. They do preliminary evaluation of projects (including estimates of the likelihood of success), and help to prepare credit applications.

Representatives of several partner institutions are members of the Warsaw Center's local advisory board. They include: Aleksander Cislak, deputy director of PKO BP Rotunda; P. Kowalski, deputy president of the Corporation of Enterprise Financing in the Polish–American Enterprise Fund; Roman Rak, president of the board of Economic Union Bank; and Jerzy Chojna, director of the credit department at the Polish Development Bank.

Cooperation with Other Groups

The Warsaw SBAC cooperates with other organizations providing education and training for small enterprises. Examples are the Polish Chamber of Commerce, local chambers of commerce, the Main School of Commerce and its College of Business Administration, the Ministry of Labor and Social Politics, the Ministry of Industry and Commerce, USAID, the US Peace Corps, the Foundation for Rural Area Water Supply, and Labor Centers.

Recently the Center started working with the Labor Center in Mokotów. Consultants will organize trainings for the unemployed with the financial sponsorship of Mokotów Community, and will consult with clients from Mokotów.

In the near future, the Center intends to cooperate with Warsaw city authorities. Special training programs are to be prepared for clients from the Labor Agency, Job Clubs, etc. The Center hopes the mayor of the city will support this effort financially.

Selected Results of Advisory and Training Activities in 1994

- STI, a company involved with production of TV programs and ads and film processing, was granted a loan for the purchase of modern equipment. The loan helped to increase the company's sales.

- The trade and service company Vispol, with help from Foundation consultants, was granted an investment credit for the sale of trucks through its leasing system.

- The entrepreneur J. Weight, from Kazimierz Wielki, had been a director of a bankrupt nationalized tourist company. With advisory help she bought up a large share of the company's assets and opened her own business, which now brings in substantial income.

- Another entrepreneur, J. Gulik, used Foundation assistance to obtain a loan for starting a health-food processing company. At present the company employs 12 people.

- A company dealing with furniture sales in Russia turned to the Foundation for help in broadening its commercial contacts in that country. Consultants helped the company find a partner with good knowledge of the Russian market. Both entrepreneurs gained profitable new contacts, and their sales increased.

- Sablex, Inc., which operates a coffee-and-peanut-roasting plant, approached the Foundation about a problem with the value added tax. The Center's director arranged a meeting between the company owner and a Ministry of Finance official responsible for VAT questions. It was decided that Sablex had been overcharged by 800 million zloty (about $33,000).

- Stalimex, a wholesaler of steel products in Plonsk, used consulting help to identify problems in its financial and accounting departments. Planning improved, and the company's turnover increased.

11 Moving Toward Sustainability: Case Studies from the Debrecen SBDC

István Bogyó
Managing Director, Debrecen SBDC

Greetings, on behalf of the Debrecen Small Business Development Center! My job here is to tell you how frenetically hard we are working and what an incredibly lot we are doing for our clients. But before introducing case studies, I would like to briefly sketch the current economic situation in Hungary.

Private Business and the Economy in Hungary

Since 1990, private ownership has become dominant in Hungary. Most of the previously state-owned companies have been privatized, and the number of businesses has skyrocketed (see Exhibit 1, Number of Businesses in Hungary). Today the number exceeds one million; thus every tenth Hungarian is a business owner!

That means 100 businesses per thousand people, which is two and a half times the rate in the developed countries of the European Union. Some researchers say this is natural, since the economic transition in Central Europe is the basis of many emerging industries and a driving force in the creation of new enterprises. The increase in the number of private businesses does not necessarily mean that we have solved our problems, but it is a key element of a successful transition to a market economy.

If we look at the distribution of these businesses by legal form, we see the majority are sole proprietorships (see Exhibit 2, Distribution of Business Types). Many of the sole proprietors are agents of multi-level marketing chains like Amway, California Fitness, and Herbalife; agents of insurance companies; agents of advertising companies; et cetera. These people are not employed by the respective companies, but are required to start their own businesses and subcontract the suppliers.

91

Another important factor is the exchange rate of the Hungarian Forint. As of March 30, 1995, one US dollar was worth 119.75 Forints, more than 20 per cent higher than a year before. No other comment on this.

Compared to 1993, Hungarian imports in 1994 grew by 24 per cent while exports grew by 21 per cent.

Foreign investments total $8.5 billion. The biggest investor is the US, with American companies responsible for 27 per cent of this amount, or $2.3 billion. The largest investments have been made by Ameritech, GE, GM, USWest, Ford, Guardian Glass, and Alcoa. Of course we must not forget Coca-Cola, Pepsi-Cola, McDonald's, and Burger King. But it is very encouraging that the largest investments are being made in innovative industries like telecommunications and automobiles. Last week it was announced that GM-Opel will invest another $140 million in the next few months. The company also announced that it wants to increase the number and contribution of Hungarian small business subcontractors.

The socialist government of Hungary recently introduced a package of laws intended to increase the revenues of the state, cut state spending, and stop corruption. The reality is more taxes and fewer jobs. The refinance interest rate at the Hungarian National Bank is currently 28 per cent which means the prime rate at banks is between 34 per cent and 36 per cent. Estimated inflation for 1995 is somewhere between 25 per cent and 30 per cent.

Crime last year was down slightly from 1993, but the 285,000 cases caused $400 million in losses for the victims.

The Debrecen SBDC

The Debrecen SBDC started in September 1992. Since then we have served more than 2,000 people with our training, counseling, and information services.

In the first part of this conference we discussed the future of these centers, and I think we all have to admit that none of us is perfectly sure what is going to happen or how things are going to happen. It is certain, though, that moving toward any kind of sustainability implies at least one drastic change in the activities of the centers: a change in the target market.

Originally these centers were set up, as the mission statement of the Debrecen SBDC mission statement puts it, 'to provide quality managerial and technical assistance to small enterprises, thereby supporting economic development throughout the service area.'

Any kind of self-sufficiency will require that the main activities be shifted toward those companies able to pay for the services. At the same time, the centers will have to face competition from established consulting companies which also have been around for a while.

Having said this, let us now take a look at how we've dealt with our clients in Debrecen. The most important activity of the Debrecen SBDC has been one-on-one counseling. As part of the counseling, we keep track of what clients think their main problems are (see Exhibit 3, Main Problems of Clients).

More than one-third say their biggest problem is the lack of capital. When we are speaking of capital, don't think of billions of dollars; in most cases just a few hundred thousand Forints are needed. But as mentioned earlier, interest rates are close to 40 per cent, and banks will not make loans to beginners or new enterprises. There are very few venture capital companies in the country, and mortgage or second-mortgage loans are practically unknown to most banks. Therefore the only reliable sources of seed capital — and to what extent they are reliable, we don't know — are family savings and loans from friends.

Another problem, cited by 20 per cent of our clients as their biggest, is lack of information. This can be information about repayable loans, about new markets, new technologies, or many other subjects. The Debrecen SBDC has compiled a tremendous amount of such information — for instance, on loan possibilities. Of course, how many of these loans are available to small businesses is another cup of tea.

To our surprise, only 2 per cent of our clients blamed other companies by saying their biggest problem is outstanding receivables. In an economy where everybody owes everybody, this is surprising indeed.

The collapse of the COMECOM still has a very negative impact on some industries, like the textile and poultry industries. For companies in these businesses it was rather difficult first to adjust themselves to the different needs of the western markets, and second to find and enter these markets. Most textile companies subcontract, thus losing most of their profits, but at least keeping their employees.

It is an environment in which some people have become very wealthy — and some very poor.

Case Studies from Debrecen

The most important fields of counseling at the Debrecen SBDC are marketing, financial assets, and business planning (see Exhibit 4, Field of Counseling). In the past year counseling on how to deal with regulations became 'popular' again, as the new government started to change all laws and regulations.

Here are some examples of assistance to clients:

• Botos Csaba had a medium-sized plot of very good land in the vicinity of Debrecen. It was not large enough for mass-production agriculture, so we recommended that he grow and sell quality seeds. He grows sunflowers.

The seeds can be easily sold, and from the first year's profits he bought a Plymouth Voyager.

- Another client worked for an automobile service station, where she was responsible for buying and selling various oils. In 1992 she realized the company was not interested in expanding, so she left to start her own business, called Kissné. With our assistance she obtained two loans, built a nice warehouse and shop, and from her high profits recently bought the neighboring shop, where she is going to sell agricultural equipment. Her core business is growing rapidly, even importing premium US motor oils like Valvoline.

- Balogh Béla inherited a large traditional house in downtown Debrecen. He literally had no idea what to do, because he had no money and no small business experience at all. He attended our series of seminars for new small business owners, learned well, and with our assistance decided to convert the house to a family-style restaurant. He is very innovative, and customers really like his creations like 'Bouillon a la Swarzenegger.'
  Of course he needed additional capital, so a loan application and a business plan were drawn up. He negotiated with three different banks and received a loan. After starting the business with his wife and one employee, today he employs eight people and his restaurant is full all day.

- Elek Laci has a transporting business, and also owns a food store which is open 24 hours a day, seven days a week. He had a business partner who cheated him badly, then left the company. Besides going to court (and the case is still not settled), he had to negotiate with the Tax Office, the Social Security Office, and suppliers in order to sustain his shop and turn the business around. After many hours of counseling and preparation, several meetings with officials resulted in his debt being suspended. He even received some benefits to help maintain his business.
  Since then he has paid his debt, the business is highly profitable, and he employs 15 people. His store sells Coca Cola, and he also was able to contract with the local wholesaler to transport Coke in Debrecen. And by the way: To make sure he is meeting customer needs, he sells Pepsi as well.

- One of our more unusual clients has found a specialty niche in the doll-furniture business: He makes furniture for Barbie dolls. It is all hand crafted of wood, and most of the products are exported to Switzerland and Germany. The SBDC helped him to find export markets and negotiate with foreign buyers.

- Another client worked for the state-owned auto sales company for many years. Wanting to benefit from his experience, he approached GM-Opel about opening a dealership in Debrecen. The deal was made, and with our aid the client submitted a successful loan application for $200,000. He built Opel Klassz Autóház, which includes service facilities and employs eight skilled people. The dealership plans to sell other GM cars soon.

- Gara Cukrászda is a traditional confectionery business. The owner wanted to expand his customer seating area, because he was able to produce far more pastries than he could sell in his limited floor space. Fortunately the neighboring bank affiliate was about to be closed, so he had the chance of a lifetime to add 100 square meters. This also would let him separate customer seating from the take-out service, and run his production at full capacity.

  With the assistance of the SBDC he applied for and received a loan of 27 million Forints. The new shop opened in March 1995 and is literally full all day. Sales are predicted to double, with profits up 50 per cent from last year.

To close this report, here is a quotation that we at the Debrecen SDBC like to use. It is a message to entrepreneurs and to all who advise and support them:

'Defeat may test you; it need not stop you. If at first you don't succeed, try another way. For every obstacle there is a solution. Nothing in the world can take the place of persistence. The greatest mistake is giving up.'

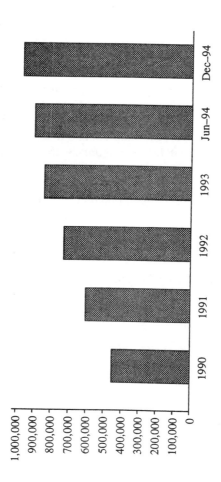

Exhibit 1
Number of Business in Hungary

Exhibit 2
Distribution of Business Types

Sole proprietorships	79.0 %
Partnerships	11.0 %
Limited liability companies	9.0 %
Cooperatives	0.8 %
Shareholding companies	0.3 %
State owned companies	0.08 %

Exhibit 3
Main Problems of Clients

Lack of capital	37.0 %
Lack of information	20.0 %
Collapsing market	13.0 %
Lack of expertise	10.0 %
Lack of ideas	3.0 %
Outstandings	2.0 %
Other	15.0 %

Exhibit 4
Field of Counseling

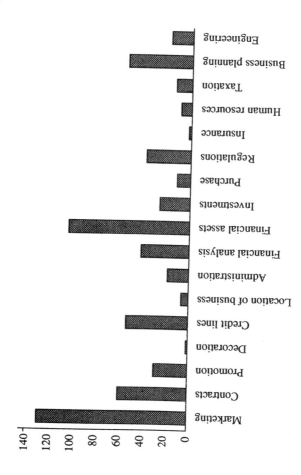

Participants in the 'Moving to Sustainability' Conference April 3-5, 1995

Czech Management Center
Celákovice, Czech Republic

Dr Catherine Ashmore
Director
International Enterprise Academy
1900 Kenny Road
Ohio State University
Columbus, OH 43210, USA

Tadeusz Aziewicz
President
Sejmik Samorzadowy Województwa Gdanskiego
ul. Okopowa 21/27
80-810 Gdansk, Poland

Mieczyslaw Bak, PhD
Vice President
Polish-American Small Business Advisory Foundation
4 Trebacka Str.
00-074 Warsaw, Poland

István Bogyó
Managing Director
Small Business Development Center of Debrecen
Péterfia u. 25
H-4026 Debrecen, Hungary

Maciej Brzeski
Deputy Mayor
Gdynia City Board
Al. Marsz. Jozefa Pilsudskiego 52/54
81-382 Gdynia, Poland

Jerzy Chojna
Acting Director
Polish Development Bank
ul. Koszykowa 54
00-675 Warsaw, Poland

Dr Mitko Dimitrov
Senior Research Fellow and Deputy Director
Bulgarian Academy of Sciences
Institute of Economics
3 Aksakov Str.
1040 Sofia, Bulgaria

Monika Edwards Harrison
Commissioner
Central European Small Business
Enterprise Development Commission
409 Third Street, S.W.
Washington, D.C. 20416, USA

Suzanne Etcheverry (University of Pittsburgh)
Director
US Agency for International Development Programs
Czech Management Center
nam. 5 kvetna 2
250 88 Celákovice, Czech Republic

Daniel S. Fogel
Commissioner, CESBEDC
Associate Dean and Professor of Business Administration
Joseph M. Katz Graduate School of Business
University of Pittsburgh
372 Mervis Hall
Pittsburgh, PA 15260, USA

Miroslav Foret
Czech Republic Small Business Development Center
Masaryk University
Zelny TrII 2/3
657 00 Brno, Czech Republic

Dr József Gellén
Chairman of the Board
Small Business Development Center of Debrecen
Peterfia u. 25
H-4026 Debrecen, Hungary

Stanislaw Ginda
Director
Polish-American Small Business Advisory Foundation
ul. Wzgórze 19 llp.
43-300 Bielsko-Biala, Poland

Ireneusz Hampel
Director
Polish-American Small Business Advisory Foundation
ul. Wiosny Ludów 6
62-500 Konin, Poland

Prof. Dr Róbert Horváth
Manager
Ybl Miklos Muszaki Foiskola
Otemetó u. 2-4
4028 Debrecen, Hungary

Frank Hoy
Chairman, CESBEDC
Dean
College of Business Adminstration
University of Texas at El Paso
El Paso, TX 79968-0545, USA

Ewa Jakubowska-Krajewska
Deputy Director, Finance and Administration
Polish-American Small Business Advisory Foundation
4 Trebacka Str.
00-074 Warsaw, Poland

Dr Katalin Kovács
Economist
Councillor of Assembly of Baranya County
Rákóczi str. 34
H-7623 Pecs, Hungary

Przemyslaw Kulawczuk
Director
Polish-American Small Business Advisory Foundation
ul. Biskupa Dominika 8
81-402 Gdynia, Poland

Jerzy Kwiatkowski
Vice Director
Polish-American Small Business Advisory Foundation
ul. Wzgórze 19 IIp.
43-300 Bielsko-Biala, Poland

Dr Jerzy Luć
Director
Polish-American Small Business Advisory Foundation
ul. Biskupa Dominika 8
81-402 Gdynia, Poland

Josephine E. Olson
Academic Dean and Interim CEO
Czech Management Center
nam. 5 kvetna 2
250 88 Celákovice, Czech Republic

Prof. Dr Bogdan Piasecki
Head of Department
Dept. of Entrepreneurship and Industrial Policy
University of Lódz
41, Rewolucji 1905 r. St.
90-214 Lodz, Poland

István Pidl
Director
Pecs Small Business Development Center
P.O. Box 55
7618 Pecs, Hungary

Tom Potocki
Chief of Party
Development Alternatives, Inc.
7250 Woodmont Ave., Suite 200
Bethesda, MD 20814, USA

Donald L. Pressley
Representative
US Agency for International Development
US AID/WARSAW
Al. Jerozolimskie 56C
Warsaw, Poland

Robert W. Pricer
Associate Director and Professor
The Enterprise Center
University of Wisconsin-Madison
5252 Grainger Hall
975 University Ave.
Madison, WI 53706-1323, USA

Ivan Shvets
Project Management Specialist
Regional USAID Mission
US Agency for International Development
US Embassy
Esplanadna 8/10, 19th Floor
Kiev, Ukraine

Andrzej Stasiek, PhD
Director
Polish American Small BusinessAdvisory Foundation
4, Trebacka Str.
III Floor, Room 316
00-074 Warsaw, Poland

Dr. István Szvitacs
Managing Director
Pollack Mihaly Muszaki Foiskola
Rókus u. 2
7624 Pecs,Hungary

Marek Szewczuk
Director
Polish-American Small Business Advisory Foundation
Lublin Small Business Development Center
Lubomelska Str. 1-3, Room 125
20-072 Lublin, Poland

Gusztáv Ványai
Counselor
Small Business Development Center of Debrecen
Peterfia u. 25
H-4026 Debrecen, Hungary

Daniel C. Wagner
Technical Advisor
Development Alternatives, Inc.
7250 Woodmont Ave., Suite 200
Bethesda, MD 20814, USA

James R. Wingrove
Executive Officer
CESBEDC
Small Business Administration
409 Third Street, S.W.
Washington, D.C. 20416, USA